Calvin's *Institutes*

Abridged Edition

Calvin's *Institutes*
Abridged Edition

Donald K. McKim, editor

Westminster John Knox Press
Louisville, Kentucky

Book design by Sharon Adams
Cover design by Lisa Buckley

First edition
Published by Westminster John Knox Press
Louisville, Kentucky

This book is printed on acid-free paper that meets the American National Standards Institute Z39.48 standard. ∞

PRINTED IN THE UNITED STATES OF AMERICA
01 02 03 04 05 06 07 08 09 10 — 10 9 8 7 6 5 4 3 2 1

Library of Congress Cataloging-in-Publication Data

Calvin, Jean, 1509–1564.
    [Institutio Christianae religionis. English. Selections]
    Calvin's institutes / Donald K. McKim, editor.—Abridged ed.
        p. cm.
    Includes bibliographical references and index.
    ISBN 0-664-22298-6 (pbk. : alk. paper)
    1. Reformed Church—Doctrines. 2. Theology, Doctrinal. I. McKim, Donald K. II. Title.
BX9420 .I58213 2000
230'.42—dc21   00-034940

This book is gratefully dedicated to my mentors in Calvin studies

Ford Lewis Battles—Calvin scholar without peer
Arthur Cochrane
John Gerstner
Robert Paul
Jack Rogers

Contents

Preface

It is a pleasure to offer *Calvin's Institutes: Abridged Edition* to twenty-first century readers.

My own commitment to Calvin's theology and interest in his *Institutes* has been long-standing. I bought my first copy on July 26, 1968. My pastor and friend John E. Karnes had introduced me to Calvin while I was a high school student. At the end of my freshman year of college, I had my own copy of this classic work.

My years at Westminster College, New Wilmington, Pennsylvania, enabled me to begin the study of Calvin with my superb teacher Jack Rogers. We studied Calvin's doctrine of Scripture together and this later led to our collaborating on *The Authority and Interpretation of the Bible: An Historical Approach* (Harper & Row, 1979). Those hours discussing Calvin in the study room of McGill Library are still vivid in my mind. Jack's excellent tutelage instilled in me a respect and heightened interest in Calvin and his *Institutes*.

One highlight of that Independent Study was a visit to Pittsburgh Theological Seminary and conversations with two committed Reformed scholars who read and appropriated Calvin quite differently. In the morning, Jack and I talked with John H. Gerstner, a devout adherent of the "Old Princeton" theology and its full expression in the theologies of Francis Turretin, Charles Hodge, and B.B. Warfield. In the afternoon, we discussed Calvin with Ford Lewis Battles, a Calvin scholar without peer who was translator of the Library of Christian Classics edition of Calvin's *Institutes*, the edition on which the following abridgment is based. Dr. Battles told us that he had not read Calvin in English before he began his translation work. We attended Battles' Calvin Seminar in which seminary students read and reacted to the whole of the *Institutes* within a single semester while Battles made significant comments from the immense reservoirs of his wide-ranging knowledge. Battles later wrote in the Foreword to our *Authority and Interpretation of the Bible* that he had "come to cherish the *Institutes of the Christian Religion* next only to the Scripture." The Gerstner-Battles experience dramatized ways in which Calvin's theology can be interpreted and appropriated in significantly different manners.

My subsequent seminary experience at Pittsburgh Seminary enabled me to gain further views of Calvin. Besides Gerstner and Battles from whom I learned much, the faculty then included two other outstanding Reformed scholars who also became my teachers and friends. Arthur Cochrane, an expert on the theology of Karl Barth, had a deep and abiding respect for Calvin, just as Barth did. Robert Paul, who supervised my doctoral dissertation, was an authority on Puritanism behind which in part, of course, stood John Calvin. My seminary opportunities for Calvin studies could not have been richer. It is to Ford Battles and these other mentors that I gratefully dedicate this book.

When I joined the faculty of the University of Dubuque Theological Seminary in 1981, I began regularly to offer a course on The Theology of John Calvin. Here students also read the entire *Institutes* in a semester—a true "baptism by immersion"—while I lectured on Calvin and we discussed their reaction papers. The experience was well worth the "perseverance of the saints."

Participation as vice-president and president of the Calvin Studies Society, attendance at Calvin conferences, International Congresses on Calvin Research, as well as writing books and articles on Calvin have kept me turning to the *Institutes* through the years. It remains a foundational work for my own theological understanding and commitment as a Reformed theologian. For all these experiences, I am thankful.

I am also deeply grateful to my wonderful family. My wife, LindaJo, and our sons, Stephen and Karl, have stuck with me through the zigs and zags of life, always loving and caring for me as they convey the grace of God. They bless me and are my joy!

I also would like to thank Davis Perkins and Richard Brown of Westminster John Knox Press who asked me to undertake this abridged edition of Calvin's *Institutes*. I greatly value their friendship and support. I worked on this project intensely in a short period of time, an effort that has been personally rewarding.

Donald K. McKim
Germantown, Tennessee
February 25, 2000

Foreword

What follows is an "abridged edition" of Calvin's *Institutes of the Christian Religion*. It is based on Calvin's 1559 *Institutes* in the Library of Christian Classics edition (LCC 20 and LCC 21) edited by John T. McNeill and translated by Ford Lewis Battles (Philadelphia: Westminster Press, 1960). The 1559 *Institutes* was written in Latin.

Since its publication in the sixteenth century, Calvin's 1559 *Institutes* has been translated into English four times. Thomas Norton translated it in 1561; John Allen in 1813; and Henry Beveridge in 1845 before the Battles translation in 1960.

Abridgments of the book have appeared through the centuries as well. The need for such works is due to what McNeill called "the cumbrous bulk" of the *Institutes* (LCC 20: xlviii).

The abridgment in English that has served most notably was first published in 1939 by Hugh Thomson Kerr as *A Compend of the Institutes of the Christian Religion* (reprint, Philadelphia: Westminster Press, 1964). It was based on Allen's translation, which had been published by the Presbyterian Board of Christian Education. Fifty years later, Kerr issued a revised work based on the LCC translation as *Calvin's Institutes: A New Compend* (Louisville: Westminster John Knox Press, 1989). An abridgment by Tony Lane with a simplifying and modernizing of Beveridge's translation by Hilary Osborne (Grand Rapids: Baker Book House, 1986) has also appeared.

Mention should also be made of Ford Lewis Battles with John Walchenbach, *Analysis of the Institutes of the Christian Religion of John Calvin* (Grand Rapids: Baker Book House, 1980). Battles provided an outline of each section of the work using the headings of his LCC translation but summarizing the contents of sections in his own words. The work is "analytical" in that it includes Battles' renderings of the main point of each section.

So the following abridgment of the 1559 *Institutes* is only one of the few major efforts to present this work of Calvin's in English in the past 200 years and one of the several efforts in the past 439 years since the Norton translation of 1561.

The Kerr *Compend* has been quite useful in the preparation of this work. At a number of points the texts I've selected on my own match Kerr's choices. At other points, I've included varying materials. The main difference between our works is that I have maintained the chapter and section headings of the *Institutes* as the framework for this book where Kerr's *Compend*, while following Calvin's order, is arranged by Kerr's own topic heads and does not account for the parts of the *Institutes* with which he does not deal. This is certainly fine and legitimate—and the popularity of this *Compend* for a half century and more attests to the usefulness of this approach.

The current abridgment, however, is more of a "road map" to the *Institutes*. It provides a picture of the whole structure of the book. It accounts for all the topics with which Calvin dealt in the course of his eighty chapters. In this way, the historical integrity of the work is maintained. Readers get a "macro" view of the whole shape of the *Institutes* as well as a "micro" view in the selections from Calvin chosen for inclusion.

Citations from the *Institutes* are typically given by three numbers: book, chapter, and section. Thus book three, chapter twenty-one, section 1 is rendered as "3.21.1" (a section on the doctrine of election). The LCC edition frequently provides headings for groups of sections that deal with a specific topic: for example, "Incidents illustrating forgiveness within the community of believers" for 4.1.23–29. I have maintained all these section summaries in the following abridged text. These particular headings and section summaries are features of the LCC edition and not of Calvin's original work. The chapter titles are Calvin's own. Usually there is a text selection from one or more of the sections cited. These are provided in Calvin's own words. But even when no text is selected, having the section summary topics shows the reader what Calvin is discussing in those sections and if interest warrants, the full edition of the *Institutes* can be consulted. So, while every individual section of the *Institutes* is not accounted for, the flow of the work can be easily traced by following the chapter titles, section summaries, and topics of each section. In this way, the full panoply of Calvin's labors here can be discerned. I hope this approach will enhance the usefulness of this volume as an abridged text. Readers can gain a wider sense of the whole work, rather than only seeing the texts selected.

In my judgment, the texts selected reflect the essential Calvin.

Some texts are a whole section; some summarize a section. Some tantalize by providing a window to Calvin's argument in a section, perhaps luring the reader to a fuller look in the unabridged version. Other section selections are important quotations from Calvin but may not directly focus on the section heading. I have included these as illuminating for Calvin's thought even as they occur, at some times tangentially, in the midst of his topic of discussion.

For the most part, the entire sections that have been omitted deal with Calvin's numerous polemical concerns. These have an importance in their own right, but they cannot in themselves claim to form the central kernel of Calvin's theology. Also generally omitted are many sections composed of the interweaving of biblical citations to buttress particular points. Calvin constantly referred to Scripture. He believed that by presenting his doctrinal discussions in the *Institutes* he did not have to prove such points when he came to writing his commentaries. Ideally, a cross-referencing of *Institutes* and Calvin's commentaries would provide the deepest view of his thought.

Past abridgments have varied in their approaches. Edmund Bunney's *Institutionis Christianae Religionis . . . Compendiously Abridged by Edmund Bunney* (1576; English translation, Edward May, *The Institutions of Christian Religion . . . [1580]*) was an abridgment of Calvin mainly in Bunney's own words. William Delaune's *Institutionis Christianae Religionis . . . Epitome* (1583) maintained Calvin's language and introduced the work with twenty-one unnumbered pages of a "General Table" of the course of Calvin's argument. This table became the source for "One-Hundred Aphorisms," which summarized the *Institutes* and which were printed with a number of later editions. Delaune's work was translated into English by Christopher Fetherstone in 1585. McNeill noted that "as a presentation of the *Institutes* in brief, it must have been a godsend to the hard-pressed student or the eager reader with limited time" (LCC 20:xlix). Other abridgments of selected amounts of the *Institutes* as well as different approaches to abridgment have followed in various languages.

I have maintained the LCC text as it has stood for forty years. Unfortunately, it does not provide inclusivity in its translation of language about humanity. This reminds us of the contextual character of all theology, as well as of all translations.

The textual apparatus and critical notes of the LCC text also have been omitted. The abbreviations that still show up are the letter "p" after a bracketed Scripture reference to indicate a paraphrase. "Vg" refers to the Latin Vulgate translation of Scripture while "Comm." stands for Calvin's commentaries. The ellipses indicate the omission of text.

The limitations of an "abridgment" are apparent. Yet this "portable Calvin" can serve useful purposes, I believe. It can be a gateway to the full text of the *Institutes* and perhaps draw a previously disinterested reader into the full richness of Calvin's important work. Kerr wrote of his *Compend* that if it "succeeds in directing some to the original, that would be warrant enough for its appearance; if it serves to introduce others to the great evangelical doctrines of the Reformation, that would be even more desirable" (*New Compend*, 14). I fully concur with Kerr's sentiments in my hopes for this volume.

In our fast-paced world of the twenty-first century, perhaps this volume can do for Calvin what the Lord prescribed to the prophet Habakkuk centuries ago: "Write the vision; make it plain on tablets, so that a runner may read it" (Hab. 2:2). May this "road map" to the *Institutes* benefit ongoing generations of students and all those interested in the theology of the Master of Geneva, John Calvin.

Introduction

John Calvin's *Institutes of the Christian Religion* has long been a theological classic. Its clarity of thought, vigor of expression, and theological acuity made it an authoritative work during Calvin's lifetime. Its enduring spiritual power to nurture the church's life and to provide a framework by which individual Christians can understand their faith has made its legacy one of abiding influence. Calvin's *Institutes* has been often translated, widely disseminated, and produced in various versions as it has significantly shaped Reformed theology and informed the understandings of generations of Christians.[1]

DEVELOPMENT OF THE INSTITUTES

John Calvin (1509–64) produced the first edition of his *Institutes* in Basel in 1536 as the *Christianae religionis institutio* or *Institution of the Christian Religion.*[2] That work had six chapters.[3] The first three were

[1]On Reformed theology see Donald K. McKim, ed., *Encyclopedia of the Reformed Faith* (Louisville: Westminster John Knox Press, 1992) and John H. Leith, *An Introduction to the Reformed Tradition*, rev. ed. (Atlanta: John Knox Press, 1981). Cf. Robert Benedetto, Darrell L. Guder, and Donald K. McKim, *Historical Dictionary of Reformed Churches* (Lanham, Md.: Scarecrow Press, 1999).

[2]The full Latin title is translated in English as *Institution of the Christian Religion Embracing almost the whole sum of piety & whatever is necessary to know the doctrine of salvation: A work most worthy to be read by all persons zealous for piety, and recently published. Preface to the most Christian King of France. Whereas this book is offered to him as a confession of faith.* John Calvin of Noyon, Author. At Basel M.D.XXXVI. See the edition translated and annotated by Ford Lewis Battles as the *Institution of the Christian Religion* (Atlanta: John Knox Press, 1975). This work was reprinted in a revised edition as John Calvin, *Institutes of the Christian Religion 1536 Edition* (Grand Rapids: The H.H. Meeter Center for Calvin Studies and William B. Eerdmans Publishing Co., 1986). The Latin word *Institutio* has the sense of "instruction" or "education."

[3]See Ford Lewis Battles, "The First Edition of the *Institutes of the Christian Religion*

its center and dealt with the Ten Commandments, the Apostles' Creed, and the Lord's Prayer.4 Successive editions followed in Latin and in French.5

The title of the 1539 edition was changed to *Institutio Christianae Religionis, Institutes of the Christian Religion*, differentiating it from the 1536 edition as it also moved from six to seventeen chapters. A number of references to early church theologians were added and Scripture citations multiplied.

By the definitive 1559 Latin edition, the work had grown to eighty chapters, organized around the articles of the Apostles' Creed—God, Christ, Holy Spirit, Church—and divided into four "books." In his "John Calvin to the Reader," Calvin wrote that despite additions and enrichments made to the editions throughout twenty-three years, "I was never satisfied until the work had been arranged in the order now set forth."6 It was his purpose, Calvin now wrote,

> to prepare and instruct candidates in sacred theology for the reading of the divine Word, in order that they may be able both to have easy access to it and to advance in it without stumbling. For I believe I have so embraced the sum of religion in all its parts, and have arranged it in such an order, that if anyone rightly grasps it, it will not be difficult for him to determine what he ought especially to seek in Scripture, and to what end he ought to relate its contents.7

(1536)" in *Interpreting John Calvin*, ed. Robert Benedetto (Grand Rapids: Baker Book House, 1996), chap. 3.

4The last three were on the Sacraments, the Five False Sacraments, and Christian Freedom. Both Aquinas in his *Compendium of Theology* (1273) and Luther in his *Small Catechism* (1529) had used the same threefold structure of Law (Ten Commandments), Faith (Apostles' Creed), and Prayer (Lord's Prayer) in their works. Augustine's *Enchiridion* (421) had as its subtitle: "Of Faith [Apostles' Creed], Hope [Lord's Prayer], and Love [Ten Commandments]." See Hugh T. Kerr, *Calvin's Institutes: A New Compend*, ed. Hugh T. Kerr (Louisville, Ky.: Westminster John Knox Press, 1989), 11.

5See the listing of editions in John Calvin, *Institutes of the Christian Religion*, ed. John T. McNeill, trans. Ford Lewis Battles, Library of Christian Classics, 2 vols. (Philadelphia: Westminster Press, 1960), Bibliography I as well as the "Introduction" to this edition written by John T. McNeill; hereafter *Inst.* Cf. B.B. Warfield, "On the Literary History of Calvin's Institutes," in *Institutes of the Christian Religion* by John Calvin, trans. John Allen, 2 vols. (Philadelphia: Presbyterian Board of Christian Education, 1936). Warfield's essay was written for the 1909 edition of this translation, produced to commemorate the four hundredth anniversary of Calvin's birth. For Ford Battles' reflections about the task of translating the LCC edition, see Ford Lewis Battles, "Englishing the Institutes of John Calvin," *Babel*, 9, nos. 1–2 (1963): 94–98.

6"John Calvin to the Reader," in *Inst.*, 3.

7"John Calvin to the Reader," in *Inst.*, 4.

THE NATURE OF CALVIN'S THEOLOGY IN THE INSTITUTES

The last four centuries have seen stupendous changes and developments in all aspects of human existence. So, too, in the field of Christian theology. Yet Calvin's theological thought endures. His successors developed theological systems and textbooks much more complex and detailed than Calvin's *Institutes*.[8] Those who followed in Calvin's theological wake built on his work to develop structures of theological thought appropriate for their times and contexts.[9] The question of the relationship between these later followers and the master himself continues to provoke debate. Yet all those in the Reformed theological tradition ultimately turn their gaze back to the Geneva reformer and to his *Institutes* as a foundational starting point.[10]

What characterizes the theology we find in Calvin's *Institutes*? Unlike some contemporary theology, the task of theological understanding was, for Calvin, an intensely personal and existential work. The *Institutes* was written for the church, for theological students, and for ordinary Christians.[11] Calvin wrote in Latin, the language of the learned in his day. The French translations that followed the Latin enlargements of the work through the years were for the benefit of the common folk who spoke the French language, Calvin's native tongue. His concern was that theology be accessible and useful.

[8]A prime example is Francis Turretin, *Institutes of Elenctic Theology*, trans. George Musgrave Giger, ed. James T. Dennison, Jr., 3 vols. (Phillipsburg, N.J.: Presbyterian and Reformed Publishing Co., 1992–97.) Turretin (1623–87) taught at the Academy of Geneva about one hundred years after Calvin's death. Cf. the selections from Reformed theologians in Heinrich Heppe, *Reformed Dogmatics: Set Out and Illustrated from the Sources*, rev. and ed. Ernst Bizer, trans. G.T. Thomson (repr., Grand Rapids: Baker Book House, 1978).

[9]This period of theological development after Calvin's death and into the seventeenth century is often referred to as Reformed Orthodoxy. See Richard A. Muller, "Reformed Orthodoxy" in *Encyclopedia of the Reformed Faith*, ed. Donald K. McKim (Louisville, Ky.: Westminster John Knox Press, 1992), 265–69.

[10]The South African Reformed theologian John De Gruchy quotes James M. Gustafson when he wrote that "Calvin remains the 'decisive generating source' for doing Reformed theology." Indeed, De Gruchy argues that "much Reformed theology, not least as articulated by John Calvin, is in critical solidarity with contemporary forms of liberation theology, and in some respects is their prototype." See his "Toward a Reformed Theology of Liberation," *Toward the Future of Reformed Theology: Tasks, Topics, Traditions*, ed. David Willis and Michael Welker (Grand Rapids: Wm. B. Eerdmans Publishing Co., 1999), 106, 108.

[11]Calvin noted in his "John Calvin to the Reader" of August 1, 1559, that "last winter when I thought the quartan fever was summoning me to my death, the more the disease pressed upon me the less I spared myself, until I could leave a book behind me that might, in some measure, repay the generous invitation of godly men." Through it all, he said he had "great zeal and effort to carry out this task for God's church," *Inst.*, 3.

Christian theology engages the whole person. The task of doing Christian theology is not an intellectual exercise alone. It is, at its root, a response to the life-giving call of God in Jesus Christ to love the Lord our God with all our heart, soul, mind, and strength (Mark 12:30). The theologian brings the best intellectual tools possible. The goal of theology in the *Institutes* is the "knowledge of God" as creator and redeemer. But as Calvin enjoins: "We are called to a knowledge of God: not that knowledge which, content with empty speculation, merely flits in the brain, but that which will be sound and fruitful if we duly perceive it, and if it takes root in the heart."[12] Knowledge of God involves trust and reverence. This knowledge comes through the gift of faith by the work of the Holy Spirit.[13] For Calvin, "no one can well perceive the power of faith unless he feels it by experience in his heart."[14] So our total selves respond to the knowledge of God we have been given and which is found in Jesus Christ.

When we read Calvin's *Institutes* we see the characteristics of Calvin's theology:

1. *Dynamic Theology.* Calvin sought always to be a "theologian under the Word of God." For him, God's revelation in the Holy Scriptures, focused on Jesus Christ, is the place from which theological understanding emerges.[15] Calvin's life was given to the interpretation of Scripture. All his writings are grounded in the dynamic interplay between God's Word of revelation and the listening ear of the church and the biblical interpreter. The dynamism of Calvin's theological thought takes shape as he hears the biblical message and understands its meaning for the church's life in his own historical context. The *Institutes* is "alive" because Calvin wants to understand and appropriate God's self-communication in life. As Calvin wrote, "Since I undertook the office of teacher in the church, I have had no other purpose than to benefit the church by maintaining the pure doctrine of godliness."[16] The living God has been revealed, and in the *Institutes* Calvin seeks to hear and obey God's Word.

---

[12]*Inst.* 1.5.9.

[13]*Inst.* 1.2.2; 3.1.4.

[14]*Inst.* 3.20.12; 3.2.36. This is the experience of "piety," which for Calvin is "that reverence joined with love of God which the knowledge of his benefits induces," *Inst.* 1.2.1. See *The Piety of John Calvin: An Anthology Illustrative of the Spirituality of the Reformer*, ed. and trans. Ford Lewis Battles, music ed. Stanley Tagg (Grand Rapids: Baker Book House, 1978).

[15]On Calvin's view of Scripture see Jack B. Rogers and Donald K. McKim, *The Authority and Interpretation of the Bible: An Historical Approach* (Eugene, Ore.: Wipf & Stock Publishers, 1999), 89–116, and Donald K. McKim, "Calvin's View of Scripture," *Readings in Calvin's Theology*, ed. Donald K. McKim (Eugene, Ore.: Wipf & Stock Publishers, 1998), 43–68.

[16]"John Calvin to the Reader," *Inst.*, 4.

2. *Evolving Theology*. The increasing size of the *Institutes* through its various editions over nearly a quarter of a century indicates that Calvin continued to hear and appropriate more of God's revelation as he developed his theological thought. A twentieth-century theologian, Carlyle Marney, once said that "theology never unpacks its bags and stays." Calvin exemplified the ways by which theology can grow as he matured and refined his understandings. His growth came through continual reading in the early church theologians, in Scripture, and in the history of biblical exegesis so that his theological judgments were not formed or articulated in an "ivory tower" vacuum.[17] Along with the development of the *Institutes* through the years came Calvin's sermons and biblical commentaries reflecting his continual wrestling with Scripture and his progressive understandings of it. Calvin's *Institutes* conveys his evolving theology.

3. *Interactive Theology*. Calvin's dynamic, evolving theology was also an interactive theology. His thought was in continual confrontation and often conflict with other views he rejected. There are long segments in the *Institutes* devoted to polemics against various groups and theological understandings from the days of the early church to his own times. In particular, Calvin wanted to distinguish his views from those of the Roman Catholic Church, Anabaptists, Schoolmen, Manichees and a host of other opponents. Calvin realized that his theology had to take into account the views of others—views with which he often pointedly disagreed. While some may find the sharpness of his polemical attacks as shocking to the sensibilities of modern times, these were standard fare in theological matters for Calvin's day. There is no denying that his vivid expressions frequently raised the temperature of theological debate.[18] Yet Calvin's arguments against his opponents helped to set his own theological course which often emerged as a "middle way" against what he considered to be "false extremes."[19]

---

[17]David Steinmetz has pointed out the importance of seeing Calvin's work as a dialogue with the whole history of the exegesis of Scripture and how our understandings of Calvin can be greatly enriched when this dimension is brought forward. See David C. Steinmetz, *Calvin in Context* (New York: Oxford University Press, 1995). For Calvin's biblical interpretation see David L. Puckett, "John Calvin," in *Historical Handbook of Major Biblical Interpreters*, ed. Donald K. McKim (Downers Grove, Ill.: InterVarsity Press, 1998), 171–79.

[18]Among the host of descriptors used by Calvin in the *Institutes* are "the mad schools of wranglers" (3.2.43); and "the foul grunting of these swine" (3.23.12).

[19]This view has been proposed by Ford Lewis Battles in "*Calculus Fidei: some Ruminations on the Structure of the Theology of John Calvin*," in *Interpreting John Calvin*, chap. 5. Cf. Donald K. McKim, "The Calvinian Works of Ford Lewis Battles" in *Interpreting John Calvin*, 35–38, and Donald K. McKim, "John Calvin: A Theologian for an Age of Limits" in *Readings in Calvin's Theology*, 291–310.

Spiritual Biography in Systematic Form

A final perspective is also important for reading and understanding Calvin's *Institutes*. Ford Lewis Battles has written that

> if we come to Calvin's *Institutes* as a source book for sys-
> tematic theology, as many have done, it will afford us valu-
> able insights indeed. But in such a reading we come to
> know but half the man. Suppose, even before we open to
> the first page, we are told: You are about to share in one of
> the classic experiences of Christian history; on the decep-
> tively orderly and seemingly dispassionate pages that fol-
> low are imprinted one man's passionate responses to the
> call of Christ. If we keep ever before us that autobiograph-
> ical character of this book, the whole man will speak to us
> in very truth.[20]

Calvin's own life, his struggles with church reform in Geneva, his polemics, his prodigious output of sermons, lectures, commentaries, and theological writings of all sorts, to say nothing of his intense involvement with the city of Geneva itself—all these elements of Calvin's autobiography are gathered together in the pages of the *Institutes*.[21] For here Calvin seeks to understand Holy Scripture and to convey God's truth to the world so that God's rule will be acknowl-edged: God reigns![22] To know this God in reverence, trust, piety and love—is the purpose of all life. For, "it will not suffice simply to hold that there is One whom all ought to honor and adore, unless we are also persuaded that he is the fountain of every good, and that we must seek nothing elsewhere than in him."[23] Calvin's own life, dedi-

---

[20]Ford Lewis Battles, "Introduction" in Ford Lewis Battles assisted by John Walchenbach, *Analysis of the* Institutes of the Christian Religion of John Calvin (Grand Rapids: Baker Book House, 1980), 14.

[21]On Calvin's life and work see William J. Bouwsma, *John Calvin: A Sixteenth-Century Portrait* (New York: Oxford University Press, 1987); Alexandre Ganoczy, *The Young Calvin*, trans. David Foxgrover and Wade Provo (Philadelphia: Westminster Press, 1987); W. Fred Graham, *The Constructive Revolutionary: John Calvin and His Socio-Economic Impact* (Richmond: John Knox Press, 1971); T.H.L. Parker, *John Calvin* (Philadelphia: Westminster Press, 1975); and Ronald S. Wallace, *Calvin, Geneva, and the Reformation* (Grand Rapids: Baker Book House, 1988).

[22]Battles notes the "political frame" of the *Institutes*, which begins with the letter to Francis I, the French king, on behalf of persecuted evangelicals and ends with a chapter on political government (4.20). See Battles, *Analysis*, 18.

[23]*Inst.* 1.2.1. B.A. Gerrish contends that this passage which "by its very location at the beginning of the *Institutes*, must be taken as regulative for everything that fol-lows" conveys Calvin's "fundamental definition of God (or, if you prefer, his funda-mental image of God): the deity is *fons omnium bonorum*, the spring or fountain of all good," *Grace and Gratitude: The Eucharistic Theology of John Calvin* (Minneapolis: Augs-burg Fortress, 1993), 26.

cated fully and completely to the knowledge of God and to the service of God, exemplified his piety—"reverence joined with love of God which the knowledge of his benefits induces."[24] The *Institutes* is Calvin's lived piety before God and before the world.

THE PURSUIT OF GOD'S TRUTH

The contemporary theologian Karl Barth wrote the following as a Preface to an edition of Calvin's *Institutes*:

> Unlike Luther, Calvin was not a genius, but a conscientious exegete, a strict and tenacious thinker and at the same time a theologian who was indefatigably concerned with the practice of Christian life, and life in the church. . . . He is a good teacher, of a kind which has been rare in the church—who does not hand over to an understanding reader the results of his study, but asks him to take it up and to discover new results in his footsteps. Only a Christian and a theologian who has learned in Calvin's *Institutes* to pursue the truth with which he is concerned by using his own eyes and ears can be a "Calvinist."[25]

John Calvin never intended creating followers to become "Calvinist." Indeed, he ordered that he himself be buried in an unmarked grave. But Calvin's whole life and efforts—seen here especially in his *Institutes*—were to pursue the truth of God, wherever it led him. This pursuit was possible, because he believed that God commands it. But it is also enabled because Calvin believed that God has already "pursued" us as human beings—by becoming a human being in the person of Jesus Christ who is "the way, and the truth, and the life" (John 14:6).

---

[24]*Inst.* 1.2.1.

[25]Cited in Eberhard Busch, *Karl Barth: His Life from Letters and Autobiographical Texts,* trans. John Bowden (Philadelphia: Fortress Press, 1976), 439. Barth also wrote that "in Calvin studies we cannot keep Calvin to what he once said as though he had nothing more or new to say today! His work did not simply occur then; it still occurs today. In what he once said he still speaks, saying what he once wanted to say. We may not speak merely of Calvin's historical impact; Calvin himself has an ongoing history into which we insert ourselves when we deal with him, in which we have a part to his honor or dishonor and to our own good or ill," *The Theology of John Calvin,* trans. Geoffrey W. Bromiley (Grand Rapids: Wm. B. Eerdmans Publishing Co., 1995), 7.

Book I

The Knowledge
of God the Creator

THE KNOWLEDGE OF GOD AND THAT OF OURSELVES ARE CONNECTED. HOW THEY ARE INTERRELATED

1.1

Without knowledge of self there is no knowledge of God

1.1.1

Nearly all the wisdom we possess, that is to say, true and sound wisdom, consists of two parts: the knowledge of God and of ourselves. But, while joined by many bonds, which one precedes and brings forth the other is not easy to discern. In the first place, no one can look upon himself without immediately turning his thoughts to the contemplation of God, in whom he "lives and moves" [Acts 17:28]. For, quite clearly, the mighty gifts with which we are endowed are hardly from ourselves; indeed, our very being is nothing but subsistence in the one God. Then, by these benefits shed like dew from heaven upon us, we are led as by rivulets to the spring itself. Indeed, our very poverty better discloses the infinitude of benefits reposing in God. The miserable ruin, into which the rebellion of the first man cast us, especially compels us to look upward. Thus, not only will we, in fasting and hungering, seek thence what we lack; but, in being aroused by fear, we shall learn humility. For, as a veritable world of miseries is to be found in mankind, and we are thereby despoiled of divine

1

raiment, our shameful nakedness exposes a teeming horde of infamies. Each of us must, then, be so stung by the consciousness of his own unhappiness as to attain at least some knowledge of God. Thus, from the feeling of our own ignorance, vanity, poverty, infirmity, and—what is more—depravity and corruption, we recognize that the true light of wisdom, sound virtue, full abundance of every good, and purity of righteousness rest in the Lord alone. To this extent we are prompted by our own ills to contemplate the good things of God; and we cannot seriously aspire to him before we begin to become displeased with ourselves. For what man in all the world would not gladly remain as he is—what man does not remain as he is—so long as he does not know himself, that is, while content with his own gifts, and either ignorant or unmindful of his own misery? Accordingly, the knowledge of ourselves not only arouses us to seek God, but also, as it were, leads us by the hand to find him.

1.1.2 *Without knowledge of God there is no knowledge of self*

Again, it is certain that man never achieves a clear knowledge of himself unless he has first looked upon God's face, and then descends from contemplating him to scrutinize himself. For we always seem to ourselves righteous and upright and wise and holy—his pride is innate in all of us—unless by clear proofs we stand convinced of our own unrighteousness, foulness, folly, and impurity. Moreover, we are not thus convinced if we look merely to ourselves and not also to the Lord, who is the sole standard by which this judgment must be measured. For, because all of us are inclined by nature to hypocrisy, a kind of empty image of righteousness in place of righteousness itself abundantly satisfies us. And because nothing appears within or around us that has not been contaminated by great immorality, what is a little less vile pleases us as a thing most pure—so long as we confine our minds within the limits of human corruption. Just so, an eye to which nothing is shown but black objects judges something dirty white or even rather darkly mottled to be whiteness itself. Indeed, we can discern still more clearly from the bodily senses how much we are deluded in estimating the powers of the soul. For if in broad daylight we either look down upon the ground or survey whatever meets our view round about, we seem to ourselves endowed with the strongest and keenest sight; yet when we look up to the sun and gaze straight at it, that power of sight which was particularly strong on earth is at once blunted and confused by a great brilliance, and thus we are compelled to admit that our keenness in looking upon things earthly is sheer dullness when it comes to the sun. So it happens in estimating our spiritual goods. As long as we do not look beyond the earth, being quite content with our own righteousness, wisdom, and virtue, we flatter ourselves most sweetly, and fancy ourselves all but demigods. Suppose we but once begin to raise our thoughts to God, and to ponder his nature, and how completely perfect are his righteousness, wisdom, and power—the straightedge to which we must be shaped. Then, what masquerading earlier as righteousness was pleasing in us will soon grow filthy in its consummate wickedness. What wonderfully impressed us under the name of wisdom will stink in its very foolishness. What wore the face of power will prove itself the most miserable weakness. That is, what in us seems perfection itself corresponds ill to the purity of God.

Man before God's majesty   1.1.3

Yet, however the knowledge of God and of ourselves may be mutually connected, the order of right teaching requires that we discuss the former first, then proceed afterward to treat the latter.

What It Is to Know God, and to What Purpose the Knowledge of Him Tends   1.2

Piety is requisite for the knowledge of God   1.2.1

Now, the knowledge of God, as I understand it, is that by which we not only conceive that there is a God but also grasp what befits us and is proper to his glory, in fine, what is to our advantage to know of him. Indeed, we shall not say that, properly speaking, God is known where there is no religion or piety. . . .

Although our mind cannot apprehend God without rendering some honor to him, it will not suffice to hold that there is One whom all ought to honor and adore, unless we are also persuaded he is the fountain of every good, and that we must seek nothing elsewhere than in him. . . .

I call "piety" that reverence joined with love of God which the knowledge of his benefits induces. For until men recognize that they owe everything to God, that they are nourished by his fatherly care, that he is the Author of their every good, that they should seek nothing beyond him—they will never yield him willing service. Nay, unless they establish their complete happiness in him, they will never give themselves truly and sincerely to him.

1.2.2   *Knowledge of God involves trust and reverence*

What is God? Men who pose this question are merely toying with idle
speculations. It is more important for us to know of what sort he is
and what is consistent with his nature. . . . [Y]ou cannot behold him
clearly unless you acknowledge him to be the fountainhead and
source of every good. From this too would arise the desire to cleave
to him and trust in him, but for the fact that man's depravity seduces
his mind from rightly seeking him.

For, to begin with, the pious mind does not dream up for itself any
god it pleases, but contemplates the one and only true God. And it
does not attach to him whatever it pleases, but is content to hold him
to be as he manifests himself; furthermore, the mind always exercises
the utmost diligence and care not to wander astray, or rashly and
boldly to go beyond his will. It thus recognizes God because it knows
that he governs all things; and trusts that he is its guide and protector, therefore giving itself over completely to trust in him. . . . For the
pious mind realizes that the punishment of the impious and wicked
and the reward of life eternal for the righteous equally pertain to
God's glory. Besides, this mind restrains itself from sinning, not out of
dread of punishment alone; but, because it loves and reveres God as
Father, it worships and adores him as Lord. Even if there were no hell,
it would still shudder at offending him alone.

Here indeed is pure and real religion: faith so joined with an
earnest fear of God that this fear also embraces willing reverence, and
carries with it such legitimate worship as is prescribed in the law. And
we ought to note this fact even more diligently: all men have a vague
general veneration for God, but very few really reverence him; and
wherever there is great ostentation in ceremonies, sincerity of heart is
rare indeed.

1.3   THE KNOWLEDGE OF GOD HAS BEEN
                NATURALLY IMPLANTED IN THE MINDS OF MEN

1.3.1   *The character of this natural endowment*

There is within the human mind, and indeed by natural instinct, an
awareness of divinity. This we take to be beyond controversy. To prevent anyone from taking refuge in the pretense of ignorance, God
himself has implanted in all men a certain understanding of his
divine majesty. Ever renewing its memory, he repeatedly sheds fresh
drops. Since, therefore, men one and all perceive that there is a God
and that he is their Maker, they are condemned by their own testi-

mony because they have failed to honor him and to consecrate their lives to his will.

Religion is no arbitrary invention 1.3.2

Actual godlessness is impossible 1.3.3

Men of sound judgment will always be sure that a sense of divinity which can never be effaced is engraved upon men's minds. Indeed, the perversity of the impious, who though they struggle furiously are unable to extricate themselves from the fear of God, is abundant testimony that this conviction, namely, that there is some God, is naturally inborn in all, and is fixed deep within, as it were in the very marrow. . . .

Therefore, it is worship of God alone that renders men higher than the brutes, and through it alone they aspire to immortality.

This Knowledge Is Either Smothered or Corrupted, Partly by Ignorance, Partly by Malice 1.4

Superstition 1.4.1

As experience shows, God has sown a seed of religion in all men. But scarcely one man in a hundred is met with who fosters it, once received, in his heart, and none in whom it ripens—much less shows fruit in season [cf. Ps. 1:3]. Besides while some may evaporate in their own superstitions and others deliberately and wickedly desert God, yet all degenerate from the true knowledge of him. And so it happens that no real piety remains in the world.

Conscious turning away from God 1.4.2

We see that many, after they have become hardened in insolent and habitual sinning, furiously repel all remembrance of God, although this is freely suggested to them inwardly from the feeling of nature.

We are not to fashion God according to our own whim 1.4.3

Hypocrisy 1.4.4

The Knowledge of God Shines Forth in the Fashioning of the Universe and the Continuing Government of It 1.5

(God manifested in his created works) 1.5.1–10

1.5.1   *The clarity of God's self-disclosure strips us of every excuse*

The final goal of the blessed life, moreover, rests in the knowledge of God [cf. John 17:3]. Lest anyone, then, be excluded from access to happiness, he not only sowed in men's minds that seed of religion of which we have spoken but revealed himself and daily discloses himself in the whole workmanship of the universe. As a consequence, men cannot open their eyes without being compelled to see him. Indeed, his essence is incomprehensible; hence, his divineness far escapes all human perception. But upon his individual works he has engraved unmistakable marks of his glory, so clear and so prominent that even unlettered and stupid folk cannot plead the excuse of ignorance. . . . [W]herever you cast your eyes, there is no spot in the universe wherein you cannot discern at least some sparks of his glory. You cannot in one glance survey this most vast and beautiful system of the universe, in its wide expanse, without being completely overwhelmed by the boundless force of its brightness.

1.5.2   *The divine wisdom displayed for all to see*

There are innumerable evidences both in heaven and on earth that declare his wonderful wisdom; not only those more recondite matters for the closer observation of which astronomy, medicine, and all natural science are intended, but also those which thrust themselves upon the sight of even the most untutored and ignorant persons, so that they cannot open their eyes without being compelled to witness them.

1.5.3   *Man as the loftiest proof of divine wisdom*

David, when he has briefly praised the admirable name and glory of God, which shine everywhere, immediately exclaims: "What is man that thou art mindful of him?" [Ps. 8:4]. Likewise, "Out of the mouths of babes and sucklings thou hast established strength" [Ps. 8:2]. Indeed, he not only declares that a clear mirror of God's works is in humankind, but that infants, while they nurse at their mothers' breasts, have tongues so eloquent to preach his glory that there is no need at all of other orators.

1.5.4   *But man turns ungratefully against God*

Here, however, the foul ungratefulness of men is disclosed. They have within themselves a workshop graced with God's unnumbered works and, at the same time, a storehouse overflowing with inestimable riches. They ought, then, to break forth into praises of him but are actually puffed up and swollen with all the more pride. They feel in many wonderful ways that God works in them; they are also taught, by the very use of these things, what a great variety of gifts they possess from his liberality. They are compelled to know—whether they will or not—that these are the signs of divinity; yet they conceal them within. . . .

Yet they set God aside, the while using "nature," which for them is the artificer of all things, as a cloak.

God's government and judgment   1.5.7

For in administering human society he so tempers his providence that, although kindly and beneficent toward all in numberless ways, he still by open and daily indications declares his clemency to the godly and his severity to the wicked and criminal.

God's sovereign sway over the life of men   1.5.8

In their desperate straits God suddenly and wonderfully and beyond all hope succors the poor and almost lost. . . . [W]hat are thought to be chance occurrences are just so many proofs of heavenly providence, especially of fatherly kindness. . . . And certainly however much the glory of God shines forth, scarcely one man in a hundred is a true spectator of it!

Indeed, his wisdom manifests his excellence when he dispenses everything at the best opportunity; when he confounds all wisdom of the world [cf. I Cor. 1:20]; when "he catches the crafty in their own craftiness" [I Cor. 3:19 p.; cf. Job 5:13]. In short, there is nothing that he does not temper in the best way.

We ought not to rack our brains about God;   1.5.9
but rather, we should contemplate him in his works

We ought to observe that we are called to a knowledge of God: not that knowledge which, content with empty speculation, merely flits in the brain, but that which will be sound and fruitful if we duly perceive it, and if it takes root in the heart. . . . Consequently, we know the most perfect way of seeking God, and the most suitable order, is not for us to attempt with bold curiosity to penetrate to the investigation of his essence, which we ought more to adore than meticulously to search out, but for us to contemplate him in his works whereby he renders himself near and familiar to us, and in some manner communicates himself.

1.5.11–12 *(Man nevertheless, failing to know and worship him, falls into superstition and confusion)*

1.5.11 *The evidence of God in creation does not profit us*

But although the Lord represents both himself and his everlasting Kingdom in the mirror of his works with very great clarity, such is our stupidity that we grow increasingly dull toward so manifest testimonies, and they flow away without profiting us.

1.5.12 *The manifestation of God is choked by human superstition and the error of the philosophers*

Hence arises that boundless filthy mire of error wherewith the whole earth was filled and covered. For each man's mind is like a labyrinth, so that it is no wonder that individual nations were drawn aside into various falsehoods; and not only this—but individual men, almost, had their own gods. For as rashness and superficiality are joined to ignorance and darkness, scarcely a single person has ever been found who did not fashion for himself an idol or specter in place of God. Surely, just as waters boil up from a vast, full spring, so does an immense crowd of gods flow forth from the human mind, while each one, in wandering about with too much license, wrongly invents this or that about God himself.

1.5.13–15 *(Persistent in error, we are without excuse)*

1.5.14 *The manifestation of God in nature speaks to us in vain*

It is therefore in vain that so many burning lamps shine for us in the workmanship of the universe to show forth the glory of its Author. Although they bathe us wholly in their radiance, yet they can of themselves in no way lead us into the right path. Surely they strike some sparks, but before their fuller light shines forth these are smothered.

1.5.15 *We have no excuse*

But although we lack the natural ability to mount up unto the pure and clear knowledge of God, all excuse is cut off because the fault of dullness is within us. And, indeed, we are not allowed thus to pretend ignorance without our conscience itself always convicting us of both baseness and ingratitude. . . . Therefore we are justly denied every excuse when we stray off as wanderers and vagrants even though everything points out the right way. But, however that may be, yet the fact that men soon corrupt the seed of the knowledge of God, sown in their minds out of the wonderful workmanship of nature (thus preventing it from coming to a good and perfect fruit), must be imputed to their own failing; nevertheless, it is very true that we are not at all sufficiently instructed by this bare and simple testimony which the creatures render splendidly to the glory of God.

SCRIPTURE IS NEEDED AS GUIDE AND TEACHER 1.6
FOR ANYONE WHO WOULD COME TO GOD THE CREATOR

God bestows the actual knowledge of himself upon us 1.6.1
only in the Scriptures

That brightness which is borne in upon the eyes of all men both in heaven and on earth is more than enough to withdraw all support from men's ingratitude—just as God, to involve the human race in the same guilt, sets forth to all without exception his presence portrayed in his creatures. Despite this, it is needful that another and better help be added to direct us aright to the very Creator of the universe. It was not in vain, then, that he added the light of his Word by which to become known unto salvation; and he regarded as worthy of this privilege those whom he pleased to gather more closely and intimately to himself. . . . Just as old or bleary-eyed men and those with weak vision, if you thrust before them a most beautiful volume, even if they recognize it to be some sort of writing, yet can scarcely construe two words, but with the aid of spectacles will begin to read distinctly; so Scripture, gathering up the otherwise confused knowledge of God in our minds, having dispersed our dullness, clearly shows us the true God. This, therefore, is a special gift, where God, to instruct the church, not merely uses mute teachers but also opens his own most hallowed lips.

The Word of God as Holy Scripture 1.6.2

But whether God became known to the patriarchs through oracles and visions or by the work and ministry of men, he put into their minds what they should then hand down to their posterity. At any rate, there is no doubt that firm certainty of doctrine was engraved in their hearts, so that they were convinced and understood that what they had learned proceeded from God. For by his Word, God rendered faith unambiguous forever, a faith that should be superior to all opinion. . . . Therefore, however fitting it may be for man seriously to turn his eyes to contemplate God's works, since he has been placed in this most glorious theater to be a spectator of them, it is fitting that he

prick up his ears to the Word, the better to profit. . . . Now, in order
that true religion may shine upon us, we ought to hold that it must
take its beginning from heavenly doctrine and that no one can get
even the slightest taste of right and sound doctrine unless he be a
pupil of Scripture. Hence, there also emerges the beginning of true
understanding when we reverently embrace what it pleases God
there to witness of himself. But not only faith, perfect and in every
way complete, but all right knowledge of God is born of obedience.
And surely in this respect God has, by his singular providence, taken
thought for mortals through all ages.

1.6.3   *Without Scripture we fall into error*

It is therefore clear that God has provided the assistance of the Word
for the sake of all those to whom he has been pleased to give useful
instruction because he foresaw that his likeness imprinted upon the
most beautiful form of the universe would be insufficiently effective.
Hence, we must strive onward by this straight path if we seriously
aspire to the pure contemplation of God. We must come, I say, to the
Word, where God is truly and vividly described to us from his works,
while these very works are appraised not by our depraved judgment
but by the rule of eternal truth.

1.6.4   *Scripture can communicate to us*
        what the revelation in the creation cannot

1.7   SCRIPTURE MUST BE CONFIRMED BY THE WITNESS OF THE SPIRIT.
        THUS MAY ITS AUTHORITY BE ESTABLISHED AS CERTAIN;
        AND IT IS A WICKED FALSEHOOD THAT ITS CREDIBILITY
        DEPENDS ON THE JUDGMENT OF THE CHURCH

1.7.1   *Scripture has its authority from God, not from the church*

Before I go any farther, it is worth-while to say something about the
authority of Scripture, not only to prepare our hearts to reverence it,
but to banish all doubt. . . . [T]he Scriptures obtain full authority
among believers only when men regard them as having sprung from
heaven, as if there the living words of God were heard. . . .

   But a most pernicious error widely prevails that Scripture has only
so much weight as is conceded to it by the consent of the church. As
if the eternal and inviolable truth of God depended upon the decision
of men! For they mock the Holy Spirit when they ask: Who can con-
vince us that these writings came from God? Who can assure us that

Scripture has come down whole and intact even to our very day? Who can persuade us to receive one book in reverence but to exclude another, unless the church prescribe a sure rule for all these matters? What reverence is due Scripture and what books ought to be reckoned within its canon depend, they say, upon the determination of the church.

The church is itself grounded upon Scripture   1.7.2

For if the Christian church was from the beginning founded upon the writings of the prophets and the preaching of the apostles, wherever this doctrine is found, the acceptance of it—without which the church itself would never have existed—must certainly have preceded the church. It is utterly vain, then, to pretend that the power of judging Scripture so lies with the church that its certainty depends upon churchly assent. . . . As to their question—How can we be assured that this has sprung from God unless we have recourse to the decree of the church?—it is as if someone asked: Whence will we learn to distinguish light from darkness, white from black, sweet from bitter? Indeed, Scripture exhibits fully as clear evidence of its own truth as white and black things do of their color, or sweet and bitter things do of their taste.

Augustine cannot be cited as counterevidence   1.7.3

The witness of the Holy Spirit: this is stronger than all proof   1.7.4

Credibility of doctrine is not established until we are persuaded beyond doubt that God is its Author. Thus, the highest proof of Scripture derives in general from the fact that God in person speaks in it. The prophets and apostles do not boast either of their keenness or of anything that obtains credit for them as they speak; nor do they dwell upon rational proofs. Rather, they bring forward God's holy name, that by it the whole world may be brought into obedience to him. . . . If we desire to provide in the best way for our consciences—that they may not be perpetually beset by the instability of doubt or vacillation, and that they may not also boggle at the smallest quibbles—we ought to seek our conviction in a higher place than human reasons, judgments, or conjectures, that is, in the secret testimony of the Spirit. . . . From this it is clear that the teaching of Scripture is from heaven.

Yet they who strive to build up firm faith in Scripture through disputation are doing things backwards. . . . [T]he testimony of the Spirit is more excellent than all reason. For as God alone is a fit witness of himself in his Word, so also the Word will not find acceptance in men's hearts before it is sealed by the inward testimony of the Spirit.

The same Spirit, therefore, who has spoken through the mouths of the prophets must penetrate into our hearts to persuade us that they faithfully proclaimed what had been divinely commanded.

1.7.5   *Scripture bears its own authentication*

Those whom the Holy Spirit has inwardly taught truly rest upon Scripture, and that Scripture indeed is self-authenticated; hence, it is not right to subject it to proof and reasoning. And the certainty it deserves with us, it attains by the testimony of the Spirit. For even if it wins reverence for itself by its own majesty, it seriously affects us only when it is sealed upon our hearts through the Spirit. Therefore, illumined by his power, we believe neither by our own nor by anyone else's judgment that Scripture is from God; but above human judgment we affirm with utter certainty (just as if we were gazing upon the majesty of God himself) that it has flowed to us from the very mouth of God by the ministry of men. We seek no proofs, no marks of genuineness upon which our judgment may lean; but we subject our judgment and wit to it as to a thing far beyond any guesswork!

Such, then, is a conviction that requires no reasons; such, a knowledge with which the best reason agrees—in which the mind truly reposes more securely and constantly than in any reasons; such, finally, a feeling that can be born only of heavenly revelation. I speak of nothing other than what each believer experiences within himself.

1.8   SO FAR AS HUMAN REASON GOES, SUFFICIENTLY FIRM PROOFS
           ARE AT HAND TO ESTABLISH THE CREDIBILITY OF SCRIPTURE

1.8.1–4   *(The unique majesty and impressiveness, and the high antiquity, of
           Scripture)*

1.8.1   *Scripture is superior to all human wisdom*

Unless this certainty, higher and stronger than any human judgment, be present, it will be vain to fortify the authority of Scripture by arguments, to establish it by common agreement of the church, or to confirm it with other helps. For unless this foundation is laid, its authority will always remain in doubt. Conversely, once we have embraced it devoutly as its dignity deserves, and have recognized it to be above the common sort of things, those arguments—not strong enough before to engraft and fix the certainty of Scripture in our minds—become very useful aids. . . . But our hearts are more firmly grounded when we reflect that we are captivated with admiration for

Scripture more by grandeur of subjects than by grace of language. For it was also not without God's extraordinary providence that the sublime mysteries of the Kingdom of Heaven came to be expressed largely in mean and lowly words, lest, if they had been adorned with more shining eloquence, the impious would scoffingly have claimed that its power is in the realm of eloquence alone.

Not style but content is decisive   1.8.2

As far as Sacred Scripture is concerned, however much forward men try to gnaw at it, nevertheless it clearly is crammed with thoughts that could not be humanly conceived. Let each of the prophets be looked into: none will be found who does not far exceed human measure. Consequently, those for whom prophetic doctrine is tasteless ought to be thought of as lacking taste buds.

(Refutation of objections regarding miracles and prophecy)   1.8.5–10

(Simplicity and heavenly character and authority   1.8.11
of the New Testament)

(Consent of the church, and fidelity of the martyrs)   1.8.12–13

FANATICS, ABANDONING SCRIPTURE AND FLYING OVER   1.9
TO REVELATION, CAST DOWN ALL THE PRINCIPLES OF GODLINESS

The fanatics wrongly appeal to the Holy Spirit   1.9.1

For of late, certain giddy men have arisen who, with great haughtiness exalting the teaching office of the Spirit, despise all reading and laugh at the simplicity of those who, as they express it, still follow the dead and killing letter. . . . [T]he Spirit, promised to us, has not the task of inventing new and unheard-of revelations, or of forging a new kind of doctrine, to lead us away from the received doctrine of the gospel, but of sealing our minds with that very doctrine which is commended by the gospel.

The Holy Spirit is recognized in his agreement with Scripture   1.9.2

From this we readily understand that we ought zealously to apply ourselves both to read and to hearken to Scripture if indeed we want to receive any gain and benefit from the Spirit of God. . . . He is the Author of the Scriptures: he cannot vary and differ from himself. Hence he must ever remain just as he once revealed himself there.

1.9.3   *Word and Spirit belong inseparably together*

The Holy Spirit so inheres in His truth, which He expresses in Scripture, that only when its proper reverence and dignity are given to the Word does the Holy Spirit show forth His power. And what has lately been said—that the Word itself is not quite certain for us unless it be confirmed by the testimony of the Spirit—is not out of accord with these things. For by a kind of mutual bond the Lord has joined together the certainty of his Word and of his Spirit so that the perfect religion of the Word may abide in our minds when the Spirit, who causes us to contemplate God's face, shines; and that we in turn may embrace the Spirit with no fear of being deceived when we recognize him in his own image, namely, in the Word. . . . [H]e sent down the same Spirit by whose power he had dispensed the Word, to complete his work by the efficacious confirmation of the Word. . . . [T]he Word is the instrument by which the Lord dispenses the illumination of his Spirit to believers. For they know no other Spirit than him who dwelt and spoke in the apostles, and by whose oracles they are continually recalled to the hearing of the Word.

1.10   SCRIPTURE, TO CORRECT ALL SUPERSTITION, HAS SET THE
          TRUE GOD ALONE OVER AGAINST ALL THE GODS OF THE HEATHEN

1.10.1   *The Scriptural doctrine of God the Creator*

We have taught that the knowledge of God, otherwise quite clearly set forth in the system of the universe and in all creatures, is nonetheless more intimately and also more vividly revealed in his Word. . . . [L]et it be enough to grasp how God, the Maker of heaven and earth, governs the universe founded by him. Indeed, both his fatherly goodness and his beneficently inclined will are repeatedly extolled; and examples of his severity are given, which show him to be the righteous avenger of evil deeds, especially where his forbearance toward the obstinate is of no effect.

1.10.2   *The attributes of God according to Scripture agree with those known in his creatures*

1.10.3   *Because the unity of God was also not unknown to the heathen, the worshipers of idols are the more inexcusable*

1.11   IT IS UNLAWFUL TO ATTRIBUTE A VISIBLE FORM TO GOD, AND
          GENERALLY WHOEVER SETS UP IDOLS REVOLTS AGAINST THE TRUE GOD

But the Lord forbids not only that a likeness be erected to him by a maker of statues but that one be fashioned by any craftsman whatever, because he is thus represented falsely and with an insult to his majesty.

HOW GOD IS TO BE SO DISTINGUISHED FROM IDOLS
THAT PERFECT HONOR MAY BE GIVEN TO HIM ALONE

As often as Scripture asserts that there is one God, it is not contending over the bare name, but also prescribing that nothing belonging to his divinity is to be transferred to another. From this it is also clear in what respect pure religion differs from superstition. Undoubtedly, for the Greeks the word εὐσέβεια [Gr. *eusebeia*] meaning "religion," also connotes befitting reverence. For even the blind themselves, groping in darkness, felt the need of adhering to a definite rule, to avoid the perverted honoring of God. . . . I believe that this word is opposed to giddy license; for the greater part of the world thoughtlessly seizes upon whatever is at hand, nay, even flits hither and thither. But godliness, to stand on a firm footing, keeps itself within its proper limits.

It is enough to recognize that, whenever any observances of piety are transferred to some one other than the sole God, sacrilege occurs.

IN SCRIPTURE, FROM THE CREATION ONWARD, WE ARE
TAUGHT ONE ESSENCE OF GOD, WHICH CONTAINS THREE PERSONS

1.13.1   *God's nature is immeasurable and spiritual*

The Anthropomorphites, also, who imagined a corporeal God from
the fact that Scripture often ascribes to him a mouth, ears, eyes, hands,
and feet, are easily refuted. For who even of slight intelligence does
not understand that, as nurses commonly do with infants, God is
wont in a measure to "lisp" in speaking to us? Thus such forms of
speaking do not so much express clearly what God is like as accom-
modate the knowledge of him to our slight capacity. To do this he
must descend far beneath his loftiness.

1.13.2   *The three "Persons" in God*

But God also designates himself by another special mark to distinguish himself more precisely from idols. For he so proclaims himself
the sole God as to offer himself to be contemplated clearly in three
persons. Unless we grasp these, only the bare and empty name of
God flits about in our brains, to the exclusion of the true God. Again,
lest anyone imagine that God is threefold, or think God's simple
essence to be torn into three persons, we must here seek a short and
easy definition to free us from all error. . . . [T]here are in God three
hypostases. Since the Latins can express the same concept by the
word "person," to wrangle over this clear matter is undue squea-
mishness and even obstinacy. If anyone longs to translate word for
word, let him use "subsistence." Many have used "substance" in the
same sense. Nor was the word "person" in use only among the Latins,
for the Greeks, perhaps to testify their agreement, taught that there
are three *prosōpa* in God. Although they, whether Greek or Latin,
differ among themselves over the word, yet they quite agree in the
essential matter.

1.13.3   *The expressions "Trinity" and "Person" aid*
          the interpretation of Scripture and are therefore admissible

Now, although the heretics rail at the word "person," or certain
squeamish men cry out against admitting a term fashioned by the
human mind, they cannot shake our conviction that three are spoken
of, each of which is entirely God, yet that there is not more than one
God. What wickedness, then, it is to disapprove of words that explain
nothing else than what is attested and sealed by Scripture!

It would be enough, they say, to confine within the limits of Scripture not only our thoughts but also our words, rather than scatter foreign terms about, which would become seedbeds of dissension and
strife. For thus are we wearied with quarreling over words, thus by

bickering do we lose the truth, thus by hateful wrangling do we destroy love.

If they call a foreign word one that cannot be shown to stand written syllable by syllable in Scripture, they are indeed imposing upon us an unjust law which condemns all interpretation not patched together out of the fabric of Scripture. . . . [W]e ought to seek from Scripture a sure rule for both thinking and speaking, to which both the thoughts of our minds and the words of our mouths should be conformed. But what prevents us from explaining in clearer words those matters in Scripture which perplex and hinder our understanding, yet which conscientiously and faithfully serve the truth of Scripture itself, and are made use of sparingly and modestly and on due occasion?

Limits and necessity of theological terms   1.13.5

If, therefore, these terms were not rashly invented, we ought to beware lest by repudiating them we be accused of overweening rashness. Indeed, I could wish they were buried, if only among all men this faith were agreed on: that Father and Son and Spirit are one God, yet the Son is not the Father, nor the Spirit the Son, but that they are differentiated by a peculiar quality.

Really, I am not, indeed, such a stickler as to battle doggedly over mere words. For I note that the ancients, who otherwise speak very reverently concerning these matters, agree neither among themselves nor even at all times individually with themselves. . . .

Indeed, if anxious superstition so constrains anyone that he cannot bear these terms, yet no one could now deny, even if he were to burst, that when we hear "one" we ought to understand "unity of substance"; when we hear "three in one essence," the persons in this trinity are meant. When this is confessed without guile, we need not dally over words. But I have long since and repeatedly been experiencing that all who persistently quarrel over words nurse a secret poison. As a consequence, it is more expedient to challenge them deliberately than speak more obscurely to please them.

The meaning of the most important conception   1.13.6

But laying aside disputation over terms, I shall proceed to speak of the thing itself: "Person," therefore, I call a "subsistence" in God's essence, which, while related to the others, is distinguished by an incommunicable quality. By the term "subsistence" we would understand something different from "essence." For if the Word were simply God, and yet possessed no other characteristic mark, John would wrongly have said that the Word was always with God [John 1:1]. When immediately after he adds that the Word was also God himself, he recalls us to the essence as a unity. But because he could not be with God without residing in the Father, hence emerges the idea of a subsistence, which, even though it has been joined with the essence by a common bond and cannot be separated from it, yet has a special mark whereby it is distinguished from it. Now, of the three subsistences I say that each one, while related to the others, is distinguished by a special quality. This "relation" is here distinctly expressed: because where simple and indefinite mention is made of God, this name pertains no less to the Son and the Spirit than to the Father. But as soon as the Father is compared with the Son, the character of each distinguishes the one from the other. Thirdly, whatever is proper to each individually, I maintain to be incommunicable because whatever is attributed to the Father as a distinguishing mark cannot agree with, or be transferred to, the Son.

1.13.7–13   *(The eternal deity of the Son)*

1.13.7   *The deity of the Word*

"Word" means the everlasting Wisdom, residing with God, from which both all oracles and all prophecies go forth. . . . God has so spoken that the Word might have his share in the work and that in this way the work might be common to both. But John spoke most clearly of all when he declared that that Word, God from the beginning with God, was at the same time the cause of all things, together with God the Father [John 1:1–3]. For John at once attributes to the Word a solid and abiding essence, and ascribes something uniquely His own, and clearly shows how God, by speaking, was Creator of the universe, Therefore, inasmuch as all divinely uttered revelations are correctly designated by the term "word of God," so this substantial Word is properly placed at the highest level, as the wellspring of all oracles. Unchangeable, the Word abides everlastingly one and the same with God, and is God himself.

1.13.8   *The eternity of the Word*

For as the names of God that have respect to his outward activity began to be attributed to him after the existence of his work (as when he is called Creator of heaven and earth), so piety recognizes or allows no name which intimates that anything new has happened to God in himself. . . . [T]he Word, conceived beyond the beginning of time by God, has perpetually resided with him. By this, his eternity, his true essence, and his divinity are proved.

(The eternal deity of the Spirit) 1.13.14–15

(Distinction and unity of the three Persons) 1.13.16–20

Oneness 1.13.16

"Baptize them into the name of the Father, and of the Son, and of the Holy Ghost" [Matt. 28:19 p.]. For this means precisely to be baptized into the name of the one God who has shown himself with complete clarity in the Father, the Son, and the Spirit. Hence it is quite clear that in God's essence reside three persons in whom one God is known.

Threeness 1.13.17

Again, Scripture sets forth a distinction of the Father from the Word, and of the Word from the Spirit. Yet the greatness of the mystery warns us how much reverence and sobriety we ought to use in investigating this. And that passage in Gregory of Nazianzus vastly delights me: "I cannot think on the one without quickly being encircled by the splendor of the three; nor can I discern the three without being straightway carried back to the one." Let us not, then, be led to imagine a trinity of persons that keeps our thoughts distracted and does not at once lead them back to that unity. Indeed, the words "Father," "Son," and "Spirit" imply a real distinction—let no one think that these titles, whereby God is variously designated from his works, are empty—but a distinction, not a division.

Difference of Father, Son, and Spirit 1.13.18

Nevertheless, it is not fitting to suppress the distinction that we observe to be expressed in Scripture. It is this: to the Father is attributed the beginning of activity, and the fountain and wellspring of all things; to the Son, wisdom, counsel, and the ordered disposition of all things; but to the Spirit is assigned the power and efficacy of that activity. Indeed, although the eternity of the Father is also the eternity of the Son and the Spirit, since God could never exist apart from his wisdom and power, and we must not seek in eternity a *before* or an *after*, nevertheless the observance of an order is not meaningless or superfluous, when the Father is thought of as first, then from him the Son, and finally from both the Spirit. For the mind of each human being is naturally inclined to contemplate God first, then the wisdom coming forth from him, and lastly the power whereby he executes the decrees of his plan. For this reason, the Son is said to come forth from the Father alone; the Spirit, from the Father and the Son at the same time.

1.13.19   *The relationship of Father, Son, and Spirit*

The Son is one God with the Father because he shares with the Father one and the same Spirit; and that the Spirit is not something other than the Father and different from the Son, because he is the Spirit of the Father and the Son. For in each hypostasis the whole divine nature is understood, with this qualification—that to each belongs his own peculiar quality. The Father is wholly in the Son, the Son wholly in the Father. . . . By these appellations which set forth the distinction (says Augustine) is signified their mutual relationships and not the very substance by which they are one. In this sense the opinions of the ancients are to be harmonized, which otherwise would seem somewhat to clash. Sometimes, indeed, they teach that the Father is the beginning of the Son; sometimes they declare that the Son has both divinity and essence from himself, and thus has one beginning with the Father. Augustine well and clearly expresses the cause of this diversity in another place, when he speaks as follows: "Christ with respect to himself is called God; with respect to the Father, Son. Again, the Father with respect to himself is called God; with respect to the Son, Father. In so far as he is called Father with respect to the Son, he is not the Son; in so far as he is called the Son with respect to the Father, he is not the Father; in so far as he is called both Father with respect to himself, and Son with respect to himself, he is the same God." Therefore, when we speak simply of the Son without regard to the Father, we well and properly declare him to be of himself; and for this reason we call him the sole beginning. But when we mark the relation that he has with the Father, we rightly make the Father the beginning of the Son.

1.13.20   *The triune God*

When we profess to believe in one God, under the name of God is understood a single, simple essence, in which we comprehend three persons, or hypostases. Therefore, whenever the name of God is mentioned without particularization, there are designated no less the Son and the Spirit than the Father; but where the Son is joined to the Father, then the relation of the two enters in; and so we distinguish among the persons. . . .

[T]he whole essence of God is spiritual, in which are comprehended Father, Son, and Spirit.

It would not even be useful for us to know what God himself, to test
our moderation of faith, on purpose willed to be hidden. When a certain shameless fellow mockingly asked a pious old man what God
had done before the creation of the world, the latter aptly countered
that he had been building hell for the curious.

Meanwhile let us not be ashamed to take pious delight in the works
of God open and manifest in this most beautiful theater. For, as I have
elsewhere said, although it is not the chief evidence for faith, yet it is
the first evidence in the order of nature, to be mindful that wherever
we cast our eyes, all things they meet are works of God, and at the
same time to ponder with pious meditation to what end God created
them. Therefore, that we may apprehend with true faith what it prof-
its us to know of God, it is important for us to grasp first the history
of the creation of the universe, as it has been set forth briefly by Moses
[Gen., chs. 1 and 2]. . . . God by the power of his Word and Spirit created heaven and earth out of nothing; that thereupon he brought forth
living beings and inanimate things of every kind, that in a wonderful
series he distinguished an innumerable variety of things, that he
endowed each kind with its own nature, assigned functions,
appointed places and stations; and that, although all were subject to
corruption, he nevertheless provided for the preservation of each

species until the Last Day. We shall likewise learn that he nourishes some in secret ways, and, as it were, from time to time instills new vigor into them; on others he has conferred the power of propagating, lest by their death the entire species perish; that he has so wonderfully adorned heaven and earth with as unlimited abundance, variety, and beauty of all things as could possibly be, quite like a spacious and splendid house, provided and filled with the most exquisite and at the same time most abundant furnishings. Finally, we shall learn that in forming man and in adorning him with such goodly beauty, and with such great and numerous gifts, he put him forth as the most excellent example of his works. But since it is not my purpose to recount the creation of the universe, let it be enough for me to have touched upon these few matters again in passing.

1.14.22 *The contemplation of God's goodness in his creation*
will lead us to thankfulness and trust

There remains the second part of the rule, more closely related to faith. It is to recognize that God has destined all things for our good and salvation but at the same time to feel his power and grace in ourselves and in the great benefits he has conferred upon us, and so bestir ourselves to trust, invoke, praise, and love him. Indeed, as I pointed out a little before, God himself has shown by the order of Creation that he created all things for man's sake. . . . [H]e willed to commend his providence and fatherly solicitude toward us in that, before he fashioned man, he prepared everything he foresaw would be useful and salutary for him. How great ingratitude would it be now to doubt whether this most gracious Father has us in his care, who we see was concerned for us even before we were born! How impious would it be to tremble for fear that his kindness might at any time fail us in our need, when we see that it was shown, with the greatest abundance of every good thing, when we were yet unborn! . . .

Whenever we call God the Creator of heaven and earth, let us at the same time bear in mind that the dispensation of all those things which he has made is in his own hand and power and that we are indeed his children, whom he has received into his faithful protection to nourish and educate. We are therefore to await the fullness of all good things from him alone and to trust completely that he will never leave us destitute of what we need for salvation, and to hang our hopes on none but him! We are therefore, also, to petition him for whatever we desire; and we are to recognize as a blessing from him, and thankfully to acknowledge, every benefit that falls to our share.

So, invited by the great sweetness of his beneficence and goodness, let us study to love and serve him with all our heart.

DISCUSSION OF HUMAN NATURE AS CREATED, OF THE FACULTIES OF THE SOUL, OF THE IMAGE OF GOD, OF FREE WILL, AND OF THE ORIGINAL INTEGRITY OF MAN'S NATURE

1.15

(Man's nature deformed; yet his soul bears, though almost obliterated, the image of God)

1.15.1–4

Man proceeded spotless from God's hand; therefore he may not shift the blame for his sins to the Creator

1.15.1

We must now speak of the creation of man: not only because among all God's works here is the noblest and most remarkable example of his justice, wisdom, and goodness; but because, as we said at the beginning, we cannot have a clear and complete knowledge of God unless it is accompanied by a corresponding knowledge of ourselves. This knowledge of ourselves is twofold: namely, to know what we were like when we were first created and what our condition became after the fall of Adam.

Diversity of body and soul

1.15.2

Furthermore, that man consists of a soul and a body ought to be beyond controversy. Now I understand by the term "soul" an immortal yet created essence, which is his nobler part. Sometimes it is called "spirit." For even when these terms are joined together, they differ from one another in meaning; yet when the word "spirit" is used by itself, it means the same thing as soul.

God's image and likeness in man

1.15.3

Man was created in God's image [Gen. 1:27]. For although God's glory shines forth in the outer man, yet there is no doubt that the proper seat of his image is in the soul. I do not deny, indeed, that our outward form, in so far as it distinguishes and separates us from brute animals, at the same time more closely joins us to God. And if anyone wishes to include under "image of God" the fact that, "while all other living things being bent over look earthward, man has been given a face uplifted, bidden to gaze heavenward and to raise his countenance to the stars," I shall not contend too strongly—provided it be regarded as a settled principle that the image of God, which is seen or glows in these outward marks, is spiritual. . . .

There is no slight quarrel over "image" and "likeness" when interpreters seek a nonexistent difference between these two words, except
that "likeness" has been added by way of explanation. First, we know
that repetitions were common among the Hebrews, in which they
express one thing twice; then in the thing itself there is no ambiguity,
simply man is called God's image because he is like God. Accordingly, those who thus philosophize more subtly over these terms
appear to be ridiculous. . . . [t]he likeness of God extends to the whole
excellence by which man's nature towers over all the kinds of living
creatures. Accordingly, the integrity with which Adam was endowed
is expressed by this word, when he had full possession of right understanding, when he had his affections kept within the bounds of reason, all his senses tempered in right order, and he truly referred his
excellence to exceptional gifts bestowed upon him by his Maker.

1.15.4   *The true nature of the image of God is to be derived from what Scrip-*
ture says of its renewal through Christ

Nevertheless, it seems that we do not have a full definition of "image"
if we do not see more plainly those faculties in which man excels, and
in which he ought to be thought the reflection of God's glory. That,
indeed, can be nowhere better recognized than from the restoration of
his corrupted nature. There is no doubt that Adam, when he fell from
his state, was by this defection alienated from God. Therefore, even
though we grant that God's image was not totally annihilated and
destroyed in him, yet it was so corrupted that whatever remains is
frightful deformity. Consequently, the beginning of our recovery of
salvation is in that restoration which we obtain through Christ, who
also is called the Second Adam for the reason that he restores us to
true and complete integrity. For even though Paul, contrasting the
life-giving spirit that the believers receive from Christ with the living
soul in which Adam was created [I Cor. 15:45], commends the richer
measure of grace in regeneration, yet he does not remove that other
principal point, that the end of regeneration is that Christ should
reform us to God's image. . . .

Now we are to see what Paul chiefly comprehends under this
renewal. In the first place he posits knowledge, then pure righteousness and holiness. From this we infer that, to begin with, God's image
was visible in the light of the mind, in the uprightness of the heart,
and in the soundness of all the parts. For although I confess that these
forms of speaking are synecdoches, yet this principle cannot be overthrown, that what was primary in the renewing of God's image also
held the highest place in the creation itself. . . . Now we see how

Christ is the most perfect image of God; if we are conformed to it, we are so restored that with true piety, righteousness, purity, and intelligence we bear God's image. . . .

Now God's image is the perfect excellence of human nature which shone in Adam before his defection, but was subsequently so vitiated and almost blotted out that nothing remains after the ruin except what is confused, mutilated, and disease-ridden. Therefore in some part it now is manifest in the elect, in so far as they have been reborn in the spirit; but it will attain its full splendor in heaven.

Manichaean error of the soul's emanation   1.15.5

(Opinions of the philosophers on the soul criticized in view of the fall of Adam)   1.15.6–8

Free choice and Adam's responsibility   1.15.8

Therefore God provided man's soul with a mind, by which to distinguish good from evil, right from wrong; and, with the light of reason as guide, to distinguish what should be followed from what should be avoided. . . . To this he joined the will, under whose control is choice. Man in his first condition excelled in these pre-eminent endowments, so that his reason, understanding, prudence, and judgment not only sufficed for the direction of his earthly life, but by them men mounted up even to God and eternal bliss. Then was choice added, to direct the appetites and control all the organic motions, and thus make the will completely amenable to the guidance of the reason.

In this integrity man by free will had the power, if he so willed, to attain eternal life. Here it would be out of place to raise the question of God's secret predestination because our present subject is not what can happen or not, but what man's nature was like. Therefore Adam could have stood if he wished, seeing that he fell solely by his own will. But it was because his will was capable of being bent to one side or the other, and was not given the constancy to persevere, that he fell so easily. Yet his choice of good and evil was free, and not that alone, but the highest rectitude was in his mind and will, and all the organic parts were rightly composed to obedience, until in destroying himself he corrupted his own blessings. . . .

Now we need bear only this in mind: man was far different at the first creation from his whole posterity, who, deriving their origin from him in his corrupted state, have contracted from him a hereditary taint. For, the individual parts of his soul were formed to uprightness, the soundness of his mind stood firm, and his will was free to choose the good. . . . But the reason he did not sustain man by the virtue of perseverance lies hidden in his plan; sobriety is for us the part of wisdom. Man, indeed, received the ability provided he exercised the will; but he did not have the will to use his ability, for this exercising of the will would have been followed by perseverance. Yet he is not excusable, for he received so much that he voluntarily brought about his own destruction; indeed, no necessity was imposed upon God of giving man other than a mediocre and even transitory will, that from man's Fall he might gather occasion for his own glory.

1.16   GOD BY HIS POWER NOURISHES AND MAINTAINS THE WORLD
            CREATED BY HIM, AND RULES ITS SEVERAL PARTS BY HIS PROVIDENCE

1.16.1–4   *(God's special providence asserted, against the opinions of philosophers)*

1.16.1   *Creation and providence inseparably joined*

Moreover, to make God a momentary Creator, who once for all finished his work, would be cold and barren, and we must differ from profane men especially in that we see the presence of divine power shining as much in the continuing state of the universe as in its inception. For even though the minds of the impious too are compelled by merely looking upon earth and heaven to rise up to the Creator, yet faith has its own peculiar way of assigning the whole credit for Creation to God. . . .

Faith ought to penetrate more deeply, namely, having found him Creator of all, forthwith to conclude he is also everlasting Governor and Preserver—not only in that he drives the celestial frame as well as its several parts by a universal motion, but also in that he sustains, nourishes, and cares for, everything he has made, even to the least sparrow [cf. Matt. 10:29].

1.16.2   *There is no such thing as fortune or chance*

God's providence, as it is taught in Scripture, is opposed to fortune and fortuitous happenings. Now it has been commonly accepted in all ages, and almost all mortals hold the same opinion today, that all things come about through chance. What we ought to believe concerning providence is by this depraved opinion most certainly not only beclouded, but almost buried. Suppose a man falls among thieves, or wild beasts; is shipwrecked at sea by a sudden gale; is killed by a falling house or tree. Suppose another man wandering through the desert finds help in his straits; having been tossed by the waves, reaches harbor; miraculously escapes death by a finger's breadth. Carnal reason ascribes all such happenings, whether prosperous or adverse, to fortune. But anyone who has been taught by Christ's lips that all the hairs of his head are numbered [Matt. 10:30] will look farther afield for a cause, and will consider that all events are governed by God's secret plan. And concerning inanimate objects we ought to hold that, although each one has by nature been endowed with its own property, yet it does not exercise its own power except in so far as it is directed by God's ever-present hand. These are, thus, nothing but instruments to which God continually imparts as much effectiveness as he wills, and according to his own purpose bends and turns them to either one action or another.

God's providence governs all   1.16.3

Truly God claims, and would have us grant him, omnipotence—not the empty, idle, and almost unconscious sort that the Sophists imagine, but a watchful, effective, active sort, engaged in ceaseless activity. . . .

Those who ascribe just praise to God's omnipotence doubly benefit thereby. First, power ample enough to do good there is in him in whose possession are heaven and earth, and to whose beck all creatures are so attentive as to put themselves in obedience to him. Secondly, they may safely rest in the protection of him to whose will are subject all the harmful things which, whatever their source, we may fear; whose authority curbs Satan with all his furies and his whole equipage; and upon whose nod depends whatever opposes our welfare.

The nature of providence   1.16.4

Providence means not that by which God idly observes from heaven what takes place on earth, but that by which, as keeper of the keys, he governs all events. Thus it pertains no less to his hands than to his eyes. . . .

("General" and "special" providence)

The universe is ruled by God, not only because he watches over the order of nature set by himself, but because he exercises especial care over each of his works. It is, indeed, true that the several kinds of things are moved by a secret impulse of nature, as if they obeyed God's eternal command, and what God has once determined flows on by itself. . . .

And surely they who cast over it the veil of which I spoke are themselves compelled to add, by way of correction, that many things take place under God's especial care. But they wrongly restrict this to particular acts alone. Therefore we must prove God so attends to the regulation of individual events, and they all so proceed from his set plan, that nothing takes place by chance.

1.16.5–7   *(Doctrine of special providence supported by the evidence of Scripture)*

1.16.8–9   *(Discussion of fortune, chance, and seeming contingency in events)*

1.16.8   *The doctrine of providence is no Stoic belief in fate!*

We do not, with the Stoics, contrive a necessity out of the perpetual connection and intimately related series of causes, which is contained in nature; but we make God the ruler and governor of all things, who in accordance with his wisdom has from the farthest limit of eternity decreed what he was going to do, and now by his might carries out what he has decreed. From this we declare that not only heaven and earth and the inanimate creatures, but also the plans and intentions of men, are so governed by his providence that they are borne by it straight to their appointed end.

1.16.9   *The true causes of events are hidden to us*

Yet since the sluggishness of our mind lies far beneath the height of God's providence, we must employ a distinction to lift it up. Therefore I shall put it this way: however all things may be ordained by God's plan, according to a sure dispensation, for us they are fortuitous. Not that we think that fortune rules the world and men, tumbling all things at random up and down, for it is fitting that this folly be absent from the Christian's breast! But since the order, reason, end, and necessity of those things which happen for the most part lie hidden in God's purpose, and are not apprehended by human opinion, those things, which it is certain take place by God's will, are in a sense fortuitous.

1.17   How We May Apply This Doctrine to Our Greatest Benefit

1.17.1–5   *(Interpretation of divine providence*
with reference to the past and the future)

1.17.1   *The meaning of God's ways*

Moreover, as men's dispositions are inclined to vain subtleties, any who do not hold fast to a good and right use of this doctrine can hardly avoid entangling themselves in inscrutable difficulties. Therefore it is expedient here to discuss briefly to what end Scripture teaches that all things are divinely ordained.

Three things, indeed, are to be noted. First, God's providence must be considered with regard to the future as well as the past. Secondly, it is the determinative principle of all things in such a way that sometimes it works through an intermediary, sometimes without an intermediary, sometimes contrary to every intermediary. Finally, it strives to the end that God may reveal his concern for the whole human race, but especially his vigilance in ruling the church, which he deigns to watch more closely. . . .

But we must so cherish moderation that we do not try to make God render account to us, but so reverence his secret judgments as to consider his will the truly just cause of all things. When dense clouds darken the sky, and a violent tempest arises, because a gloomy mist is cast over our eyes, thunder strikes our ears and all our senses are benumbed with fright, everything seems to us to be confused and mixed up; but all the while a constant quiet and serenity ever remain in heaven. So must we infer that, while the disturbances in the world deprive us of judgment, God out of the pure light of his justice and wisdom tempers and directs these very movements in the best-conceived order to a right end.

God's rule will be observed with respect!   1.17.2

Therefore no one will weigh God's providence properly and profitably but him who considers that his business is with his Maker and the Framer of the universe, and with becoming humility submits himself to fear and reverence. . . . Therefore, since God assumes to himself the right (unknown to us) to rule the universe, let our law of soberness and moderation be to assent to his supreme authority, that his will may be for us the sole rule of righteousness, and the truly just cause of all things.

God's providence does not relieve us from responsibility   1.17.3

All who will compose themselves to this moderation will not murmur against God on account of their adversities in time past, nor lay the blame for their own wickedness upon him. . . . But rather let them inquire and learn from Scripture what is pleasing to God so that they may strive toward this under the Spirit's guidance. At the same time, being ready to follow God wherever he calls, they will show in very truth that nothing is more profitable than the knowledge of this doctrine.

God's providence does not excuse us from due prudence   1.17.4

For he who has set the limits to our life has at the same time entrusted to us its care; he has provided means and helps to preserve it; he has also made us able to foresee dangers; that they may not overwhelm us unaware, he has offered precautions and remedies. Now it is very clear what our duty is: thus, if the Lord has committed to us the protection of our life, our duty is to protect it; if he offers helps, to use them; if he forewarns us of dangers, not to plunge headlong; if he makes remedies available, not to neglect them. . . . God's providence does not always meet us in its naked form, but God in a sense clothes it with the means employed.

1.17.5   *God's providence does not exculpate our wickedness*

Thieves and murderers and other evildoers are the instruments of divine providence, and the Lord himself uses these to carry out the judgments that he has determined with himself. Yet I deny that they can derive from this any excuse for their evil deeds. Why? Will they either involve God in the same iniquity with themselves, or will they cloak their own depravity with his justice? They can do neither. In their own conscience they are so convicted as to be unable to clear themselves; in themselves they so discover all evil, but in him only the lawful use of their evil intent, as to preclude laying the charge against God. Well and good, for he works through them.

1.17.6–11   *(Meditating on the ways of God in providence:*
            the happiness of recognizing acts of providence)

1.17.6   *God's providence as solace of believers*

Therefore the Christian heart, since it has been thoroughly persuaded that all things happen by God's plan, and that nothing takes place by chance, will ever look to him as the principal cause of things, yet will give attention to the secondary causes in their proper place. Then the heart will not doubt that God's singular providence keeps watch to preserve it, and will not suffer anything to happen but what may turn out to its good and salvation. . . .

    Indeed, the principal purpose of Biblical history is to teach that the Lord watches over the ways of the saints with such great diligence that they do not even stumble over a stone [cf. Ps. 91:12].

1.17.7   *God's providence in prosperity*

Gratitude of mind for the favorable outcome of things, patience in adversity, and also incredible freedom from worry about the future all necessarily follow upon this knowledge. Therefore whatever shall happen prosperously and according to the desire of his heart, God's servant will attribute wholly to God, whether he feels God's beneficence through the ministry of men, or has been helped by inanimate creatures. For thus he will reason in his mind: surely it is the Lord who has inclined their hearts to me, who has so bound them to me that they should become the instruments of his kindness toward me.

Certainty about God's providence helps us in all adversities   1.17.8

If anything adverse happens, straightway he will raise up his heart here also unto God, whose hand can best impress patience and peaceful moderation of mind upon us. . . . To sum this up: when we are unjustly wounded by men, let us overlook their wickedness (which would but worsen our pain and sharpen our minds to revenge), remember to mount up to God, and learn to believe for certain that whatever our enemy has wickedly committed against us was permitted and sent by God's just dispensation.

No disregard of intermediate causes!   1.17.9

Meanwhile, nevertheless, a godly man will not overlook the secondary causes. . . . [F]or benefits received he will reverence and praise the Lord as their principal author, but will honor men as his ministers; and will know what is in fact true: it is by God's will that he is beholden to those through whose hand God willed to be beneficent. If this godly man suffers any loss because of negligence or imprudence, he will conclude that it came about by the Lord's will, but also impute it to himself.

Certainty about God's providence puts joyous trust toward God in our hearts   1.17.11

When that light of divine providence has once shone upon a godly man, he is then relieved and set free not only from the extreme anxiety and fear that were pressing him before, but from every care. For as he justly dreads fortune, so he fearlessly dares commit himself to God. His solace, I say, is to know that his Heavenly Father so holds all things in his power, so rules by his authority and will, so governs by his wisdom, that nothing can befall except he determine it. . . .

Ignorance of providence is the ultimate of all miseries; the highest blessedness lies in the knowledge of it.

(Answers to objections)   1.17.12–14

Scripture speaks of God's "repentance" to make allowance for our understanding   1.17.13

What, therefore, does the word "repentance" mean? Surely its meaning is like that of all other modes of speaking that describe God for us in human terms. For because our weakness does not attain to his exalted state, the description of him that is given to us must be accommodated to our capacity so that we may understand it. Now the mode of accommodation is for him to represent himself to us not as he is in himself, but as he seems to us. . . . Meanwhile neither God's plan nor his will is reversed, nor his volition altered; but what he had from eternity foreseen, approved, and decreed, he pursues in uninterrupted tenor, however sudden the variation may appear in men's eyes.

1.18   GOD SO USES THE WORKS OF THE UNGODLY, AND SO BENDS
            THEIR MINDS TO CARRY OUT HIS JUDGMENTS, THAT
                HE REMAINS PURE FROM EVERY STAIN

1.18.1   *No mere "permission"!*

The distinction was devised between doing and permitting because to many this difficulty seemed inexplicable, that Satan and all the impious are so under God's hand and power that he directs their malice to whatever end seems good to him, and uses their wicked deeds to carry out his judgments. . . .

Yet . . . it is more than evident that they babble and talk absurdly who, in place of God's providence, substitute bare permission—as if God sat in a watchtower awaiting chance events, and his judgments thus depended upon human will.

1.18.2   *How does God's impulse come to pass in men?*

Since God's will is said to be the cause of all things, I have made his providence the determinative principle for all human plans and works, not only in order to display its force in the elect, who are ruled by the Holy Spirit, but also to compel the reprobate to obedience.

1.18.3   *God's will is a unity*

1.18.4   *Even when God uses the deeds of the godless for his purposes,
         he does not suffer reproach*

For our wisdom ought to be nothing else than to embrace with humble teachableness, and at least without finding fault, whatever is taught in Sacred Scripture.

Book II

The Knowledge of God the Redeemer in Christ, First Disclosed to the Fathers under the Law, and Then to Us in the Gospel

BY THE FALL AND REVOLT OF ADAM THE WHOLE HUMAN RACE WAS
DELIVERED TO THE CURSE, AND DEGENERATED FROM ITS
ORIGINAL CONDITION; THE DOCTRINE OF ORIGINAL SIN

(A true knowledge of ourselves destroys self-confidence)

Wrong and right knowledge of self

With good reason the ancient proverb strongly recommended knowledge of self to man. For if it is considered disgraceful for us not to know all that pertains to the business of human life, even more detestable is our ignorance of ourselves, by which, when making decisions in necessary matters, we miserably deceive and even blind ourselves! . . .

But knowledge of ourselves lies first in considering what we were given at creation and how generously God continues his favor toward us, in order to know how great our natural excellence would be if only it had remained unblemished; yet at the same time to bear in mind that there is in us nothing of our own, but that we hold on sufferance whatever God has bestowed upon us. Hence we are ever dependent on him. Secondly, to call to mind our miserable condition after Adam's fall; the awareness of which, when all our boasting and

33

self-assurance are laid low, should truly humble us and overwhelm us with shame.

2.1.3   *The two chief problems of self-knowledge*

Let us divide the knowledge that man ought to have of himself. First, he should consider for what purpose he was created and endowed with no mean gifts. By this knowledge he should arouse himself to meditation upon divine worship and the future life. Secondly, he should weigh his own abilities—or rather, lack of abilities. When he perceives this lack, he should lie prostrate in extreme confusion, so to speak, reduced to nought. The first consideration tends to make him recognize the nature of his duty; the second, the extent of his ability to carry it out.

2.1.4–7   *(Adam's sin entailed loss of man's original endowment and ruin of the whole human race)*

2.1.4   *The history of the Fall shows us what sin is [Gen., ch. 3]: unfaithfulness*

Because what God so severely punished must have been no light sin but a detestable crime, we must consider what kind of sin there was in Adam's desertion that enkindled God's fearful vengeance against the whole of mankind. . . . Adam was denied the tree of the knowledge of good and evil to test his obedience and prove that he was willingly under God's command. The very name of the tree shows the sole purpose of the precept was to keep him content with his lot and to prevent him from becoming puffed up with wicked lust. But the promise by which he was bidden to hope for eternal life so long as he ate from the tree of life, and, conversely, the terrible threat of death once he tasted of the tree of the knowledge of good and evil, served to prove and exercise his faith. Hence it is not hard to deduce by what means Adam provoked God's wrath upon himself. Indeed, Augustine speaks rightly when he declares that pride was the beginning of all evils. For if ambition had not raised man higher than was meet and right, he could have remained in his original state. . . . [D]isobedience was the beginning of the Fall. This Paul also confirms, teaching that all were lost through the disobedience of one man [Rom. 5:19]. . . . Unfaithfulness, then, was the root of the Fall. But thereafter ambition and pride, together with ungratefulness, arose, because Adam by seeking more than was granted him shamefully spurned God's great bounty, which had been lavished upon him. To have been made in the likeness of God seemed a small matter to a son of earth unless he also attained equality with God—a monstrous wickedness!

The first sin as original sin   2.1.5

As it was the spiritual life of Adam to remain united and bound to his
Maker, so estrangement from him was the death of his soul. Nor is it
any wonder that he consigned his race to ruin by his rebellion when
he perverted the whole order of nature in heaven and on earth. "All
creatures," says Paul, "are groaning" [Rom. 8:22], "subject to corruption, not of their own will" [Rom. 8:20]. If the cause is sought, there is
no doubt that they are bearing part of the punishment deserved by
man, for whose use they were created. Since, therefore, the curse,
which goes about through all the regions of the world, flowed hither
and yon from Adam's guilt, it is not unreasonable if it is spread to all
his offspring. Therefore, after the heavenly image was obliterated in
him, he was not the only one to suffer this punishment—that, in place
of wisdom, virtue, holiness, truth, and justice, with which adorn-
ments he had been clad, there came forth the most filthy plagues,
blindness, impotence, impurity, vanity, and injustice—but he also
entangled and immersed his offspring in the same miseries.

This is the inherited corruption, which the church fathers termed
"original sin," meaning by the word "sin" the depravation of a nature
previously good and pure. . . . [W]e are corrupted not by derived wickedness, but that we bear inborn defect from our mother's womb. . . .
Therefore all of us, who have descended from impure seed, are born
infected with the contagion of sin. In fact, before we saw the light of
this life we were soiled and spotted in God's sight. "For who can
bring a clean thing from an unclean? There is not one"—as The Book
of Job says [Job 14:4, cf. Vg.].

The transmission of sin from one generation to another   2.1.7

The Lord entrusted to Adam those gifts which he willed to be conferred upon human nature. Hence Adam, when he lost the gifts
received, lost them not only for himself but for us all. . . . As Augustine says, whether a man is a guilty unbeliever or an innocent
believer, he begets not innocent but guilty children, for he begets
them from a corrupted nature.

(Original sin defined as a depravity of nature,   2.1.8–11
which deserves punishment, but which is not from nature as created)

The nature of original sin   2.1.8

Original sin, therefore, seems to be a hereditary depravity and corruption of our nature, diffused into all parts of the soul, which first

makes us liable to God's wrath, then also brings forth in us those works which Scripture calls "works of the flesh" [Gal. 5:19]. And that is properly what Paul often calls sin. . . .

We must, therefore, distinctly note these two things. First, we are so vitiated and perverted in every part of our nature that by this great corruption we stand justly condemned and convicted before God, to whom nothing is acceptable but righteousness, innocence, and purity. . . .

Then comes the second consideration: that this perversity never ceases in us, but continually bears new fruits—the works of the flesh that we have already described—just as a burning furnace gives forth flame and sparks, or water ceaselessly bubbles up from a spring. . . . Those who have said that original sin is "concupiscence" have used an appropriate word, if only it be added—something that most will by no means concede—that whatever is in man, from the understanding to the will, from the soul even to the flesh, has been defiled and crammed with this concupiscence. Or, to put it more briefly, the whole man is of himself nothing but concupiscence.

2.1.9   *Sin overturns the whole man*

For this reason, I have said that all parts of the soul were possessed by sin after Adam deserted the fountain of righteousness. For not only did a lower appetite seduce him, but unspeakable impiety occupied the very citadel of his mind, and pride penetrated to the depths of his heart. . . .

That part in which the excellence and nobility of the soul especially shine has not only been wounded, but so corrupted that it needs to be healed and to put on a new nature as well. We shall soon see to what extent sin occupies both mind and heart. Here I only want to suggest briefly that the whole man is overwhelmed—as by a deluge—from head to foot, so that no part is immune from sin and all that proceeds from him is to be imputed to sin. As Paul says, all turnings of the thoughts to the flesh are enmities against God [Rom. 8:7], and are therefore death [Rom. 8:6].

2.1.10   *Sin is not our nature, but its derangement*

Now away with those persons who dare write God's name upon their faults, because we declare that men are vicious by nature! They perversely search out God's handiwork in their own pollution, when they ought rather to have sought it in that unimpaired and uncorrupted nature of Adam. Our destruction, therefore, comes from the guilt of our flesh, not from God, inasmuch as we have perished solely because we have degenerated from our original condition.

"Natural" corruption of the "nature" created by God   2.1.11

MAN HAS NOW BEEN DEPRIVED OF FREEDOM OF CHOICE AND   2.2
BOUND OVER TO MISERABLE SERVITUDE

(Perils of this topic: point of view established)   2.2.1

(Critical discussion of opinions on free will   2.2.2–9
given by philosophers and theologians)

That man is necessarily, but without compulsion,   2.2.7
a sinner establishes no doctrine of free will

Man will then be spoken of as having this sort of free decision, not
because he has free choice equally of good and evil, but because he
acts wickedly by will, not by compulsion. Well put, indeed, but what
purpose is served by labeling with a proud name such a slight thing?
A noble freedom, indeed—for man not to be forced to serve sin, yet to
be such a willing slave that his will is bound by the fetters of sin!

Augustine's doctrine of "free will"   2.2.8

Now, if the authority of the fathers has weight with us, they indeed
have the word constantly on their lips, yet at the same time they
declare what it connotes to them. First of all, there is Augustine, who
does not hesitate to call it "unfree." Elsewhere he is angry toward
those who deny that the will is free; but he states his main reason in
these words: "Only let no one so dare to deny the decision of the will
as to wish to excuse sin." Yet elsewhere he plainly confesses that
"without the Spirit man's will is not free, since it has been laid under
by shackling and conquering desires." Likewise, when the will was
conquered by the vice into which it had fallen, human nature began
to lose its freedom. Again, man, using free will badly, has lost both
himself and his will. Again, the free will has been so enslaved that it
can have no power for righteousness. Again, what God's grace has
not freed will not be free. Again, the justice of God is not fulfilled
when the law so commands, and man acts as if by his own strength;
but when the Spirit helps, and man's will, not free, but freed by God,
obeys. And he gives a brief account of all these matters when he
writes elsewhere: man, when he was created, received great powers
of free will, but lost them by sinning. Therefore in another passage,
after showing that free will is established through grace, he bitterly
inveighs against those who claim it for themselves without grace.
"Why then," he says, "do miserable men either dare to boast of free

will before they have been freed, or of their powers, if they have already been freed? And they do not heed the fact that in the term 'free will' freedom seems to be implied. 'Now where the Spirit of the Lord is, there is freedom' [II Cor. 3:17]. If, therefore, they are slaves of sin, why do they boast of free will? For a man becomes the slave of him who has overcome him."

2.2.10–11   *(We must abandon all self-approbation)*

2.2.11   *True humility gives God alone the honor*

A saying of Chrysostom's has always pleased me very much, that the foundation of our philosophy is humility. But that of Augustine pleases me even more: "When a certain rhetorician was asked what was the chief rule in eloquence, he replied, 'Delivery'; what was the second rule, 'Delivery'; what was the third rule, 'Delivery'; so if you ask me concerning the precepts of the Christian religion, first, second, third, and always I would answer, 'Humility.'"

2.2.12–17   *(Man's natural endowments not wholly extinguished: the understanding)*

2.2.15   *Science as God's gift*

Whenever we come upon these matters in secular writers, let that admirable light of truth shining in them teach us that the mind of man, though fallen and perverted from its wholeness, is nevertheless clothed and ornamented with God's excellent gifts. If we regard the Spirit of God as the sole fountain of truth, we shall neither reject the truth itself, nor despise it wherever it shall appear, unless we wish to dishonor the Spirit of God. . . . Those men whom Scripture [I Cor. 2:14] calls "natural men" were, indeed, sharp and penetrating in their investigation of inferior things. Let us, accordingly, learn by their example how many gifts the Lord left to human nature even after it was despoiled of its true good.

2.2.16   *Human competence in art and science*
also derives from the Spirit of God

Meanwhile, we ought not to forget those most excellent benefits of the divine Spirit, which he distributes to whomever he wills, for the common good of mankind. . . . But if the Lord has willed that we be helped in physics, dialectic, mathematics, and other like disciplines, by the work and ministry of the ungodly, let us use this assistance. For if we neglect God's gift freely offered in these arts, we ought to suffer just punishment for our sloths.

Summary of 12–16

To sum up: We see among all mankind that reason is proper to our nature; it distinguishes us from brute beasts, just as they by possessing feeling differ from inanimate things. Now, because some are born fools or stupid, that defect does not obscure the general grace of God. Rather, we are warned by that spectacle that we ought to ascribe what is left in us to God's kindness. For if he had not spared us, our fall would have entailed the destruction of our whole nature. Some men excel in keenness; others are superior in judgment; still others have a readier wit to learn this or that art. In this variety God commends his grace to us, lest anyone should claim as his own what flowed from the sheer bounty of God.

(But spiritual discernment is wholly lost until we are regenerated)

The limits of our understanding

We must now analyze what human reason can discern with regard to God's Kingdom and to spiritual insight. This spiritual insight consists chiefly in three things: (1) knowing God; (2) knowing his fatherly favor in our behalf, in which our salvation consists; (3) knowing how to frame our life according to the rule of his law. In the first two points—and especially in the second—the greatest geniuses are blinder than moles! Certainly I do not deny that one can read competent and apt statements about God here and there in the philosophers, but these always show a certain giddy imagination. . . . Human reason, therefore, neither approaches, nor strives toward, nor even takes a straight aim at, this truth: to understand who the true God is or what sort of God he wishes to be toward us.

Man's spiritual blindness shown from John 1:4–5

Flesh is not capable of such lofty wisdom as to conceive God and what is God's, unless it be illumined by the Spirit of God. As Christ testified, the fact that Peter recognized him was a special revelation of the Father [Matt. 16:17].

Man's knowledge of God is God's own work

It therefore remains for us to understand that the way to the Kingdom of God is open only to him whose mind has been made new by the illumination of the Holy Spirit.

2.2.22–25   *(Sin is distinct from ignorance [vs. Plato],*
but may be occasioned by delusion)

2.2.22   *The evidence of God's will that man possesses*
makes him inexcusable but procures for him no right knowledge

There is nothing more common than for a man to be sufficiently instructed in a right standard of conduct by natural law (of which the apostle is here speaking [Rom. 2:14–15—ed.]). Let us consider, however, for what purpose men have been endowed with this knowledge of the law. . . . The purpose of natural law . . . is to render man inexcusable. This would not be a bad definition: natural law is that apprehension of the conscience which distinguishes sufficiently between just and unjust, and which deprives men of the excuse of ignorance, while it proves them guilty by their own testimony.

2.2.26–27   *(Man's inability to will the good)*

2.2.27   *Our will cannot long for the good without the Holy Spirit*

But the Spirit comes, not from nature, but from regeneration. . . . We are all sinners by nature; therefore we are held under the yoke of sin. But if the whole man lies under the power of sin, surely it is necessary that the will, which is its chief seat, be restrained by the stoutest bonds. Paul's saying would not make sense, that "it is God who is at work to will in us" [Phil. 2:13 p.], if any will preceded the grace of the Spirit. Away then with all that "preparation" which many babble about! For even if believers sometimes ask that their hearts be conformed to obedience to God's law, as David in a number of passages does, yet we must also note that this desire to pray comes from God.

2.3   ONLY DAMNABLE THINGS COME FORTH
FROM MAN'S CORRUPT NATURE

2.3.1–5   *(Corruption of man's nature is such as to require*
total renewal of his mind and will)

2.3.2   *Romans, ch. 3, as witness for man's corruption*

Men are as they are here described [Rom. 3:10–16, 18—ed.] not merely by the defect of depraved custom, but also by depravity of nature. The reasoning of the apostle cannot otherwise stand: Except out of the Lord's mercy there is no salvation for man, for in himself he is lost and forsaken [Rom. 3:23 ff.].

God's grace sometimes restrains where it does not cleanse 2.3.3

But here it ought to occur to us that amid this corruption of nature there is some place for God's grace; not such grace as to cleanse it, but to restrain it inwardly. . . . [S]ome are restrained by shame from breaking out into many kinds of foulness, others by the fear of the law—even though they do not, for the most part, hide their impurity. Still others, because they consider an honest manner of life profitable, in some measure aspire to it. Others rise above the common lot, in order by their excellence to keep the rest obedient to them. Thus God by his providence bridles perversity of nature, that it may not break forth into action; but he does not purge it within.

Man sins of necessity, but without compulsion 2.3.5

Because of the bondage of sin by which the will is held bound, it cannot move toward good, much less apply itself thereto; for a movement of this sort is the beginning of conversion to God, which in Scripture is ascribed entirely to God's grace. . . . For man, when he gave himself over to this necessity, was not deprived of will, but of soundness of will. Not inappropriately Bernard teaches that to will is in us all: but to will good is gain; to will evil, loss. Therefore simply to will is of man; to will ill, of a corrupt nature; to will well, of grace. . . .

Man, as he was corrupted by the Fall, sinned willingly, not unwillingly or by compulsion; by the most eager inclination of his heart, not by forced compulsion; by the prompting of his own lust, not by compulsion from without. Yet so depraved is his nature that he can be moved or impelled only to evil. But if this is true, then it is clearly expressed that man is surely subject to the necessity of sinning.

(Conversion of the will is the effect of divine grace inwardly bestowed) 2.3.6–14

Men's inability to do good manifests itself above all 2.3.6
in the work of redemption, which God does quite alone

It behooves us to consider the sort of remedy by which divine grace corrects and cures the corruption of nature. Since the Lord in coming to our aid bestows upon us what we lack, when the nature of his work in us appears, our destitution will, on the other hand, at once be manifest. When the apostle tells the Philippians he is confident "that he who began a good work in you will bring it to completion at the day of Jesus Christ" [Phil. 1:6], there is no doubt that through "the beginning of a good work" he denotes the very origin of conversion itself, which is in the will. God begins his good work in us, therefore, by

arousing love and desire and zeal for righteousness in our hearts; or,
to speak more correctly, by bending, forming, and directing, our
hearts to righteousness. He completes his work, moreover, by confirming us to perseverance. . . .

2.3.7   *It is not a case of the believer's "co-operation" with grace;*
         the will is first actuated through grace

But perhaps some will concede that the will is turned away from the
good by its own nature and is converted by the Lord's power alone,
yet in such a way that, having been prepared, it then has its own part
in the action. As Augustine teaches, grace precedes every good work;
while will does not go before as its leader but follows after as its attendant. . . . But I contend that in the words of the prophet that I have
cited, as well as in other passages, two things are clearly signified: (1)
the Lord corrects our evil will, or rather extinguishes it; (2) he substi-
tutes for it a good one from himself. In so far as it is anticipated by
grace, to that degree I concede that you may call your will an "attendant." But because the will reformed is the Lord's work, it is wrongly
attributed to man that he obeys prevenient grace with his will as
attendant. Therefore Chrysostom erroneously wrote: "Neither grace
without will nor will without grace can do anything." As if grace did
not also actuate the will itself, as we have just seen from Paul [cf. Phil.
2:13]! Nor was it Augustine's intent, in calling the human will the
attendant of grace, to assign to the will in good works a function second to that of grace. His only purpose was, rather, to refute that very
evil doctrine of Pelagius which lodged the first cause of salvation in
man's merit.

    Enough for the argument at hand, Augustine contends, was the
fact that grace is prior to all merit. . . . [H]e makes God himself wholly
the Author of good works.

2.3.8   *Scripture imputes to God all that is for our benefit*

Surely there is ready and sufficient reason to believe that good takes
its origin from God alone. And only in the elect does one find a will
inclined to good. Yet we must seek the cause of election outside men.
It follows, thence, that man has a right will not from himself, but that
it flows from the same good pleasure by which we were chosen before
the creation of the world [Eph. 1:4]. Further, there is another similar
reason: for since willing and doing well take their origin from faith,
we ought to see what is the source of faith itself.

    But since the whole of Scripture proclaims that faith is a free gift of

God, it follows that when we, who are by nature inclined to evil with our whole heart, begin to will good, we do so out of mere grace.

The prayers in Scripture especially show how the beginning, 2.3.9
continuation, and end of our blessedness come from God alone

The first part of a good work is will; the other, a strong effort to accomplish it; the author of both is God. Therefore we are robbing the Lord if we claim for ourselves anything either in will or in accomplishment.

Perseverance is exclusively God's work; 2.3.11
it is neither a reward nor a complement of our individual act

For after [Paul] had said, "It is God who works in us to will and to accomplish," he went on to say that he does both "for his good pleasure" [Phil. 2:13 p.]. By this expression he means that God's loving-kindness is freely given. To this, our adversaries usually say that after we have accepted the first grace, then our own efforts co-operate with subsequent grace. To this I reply: If they mean that after we have by the Lord's power once for all been brought to obey righteousness, we go forward by our own power and are inclined to follow the action of grace, I do not gainsay it. For it is very certain that where God's grace reigns, there is readiness to obey it. Yet whence does this readiness come? Does not the Spirit of God, everywhere self-consistent, nourish the very inclination to obedience that he first engendered, and strengthen its constancy to persevere? Yet if they mean that man has in himself the power to work in partnership with God's grace, they are most wretchedly deluding themselves.

Augustine does not eliminate man's will, 2.3.14
but makes it wholly dependent upon grace

Elsewhere he says that will is not taken away by grace, but is changed from evil into good, and helped when it is good. By this he means only that man is not borne along without any motion of the heart, as if by an outside force; rather, he is so affected within that he obeys from the heart. . . . But the matter cannot be summed up in briefer form than in the eighth chapter of the book *On Rebuke and Grace to Valentinus.* There Augustine first teaches: the human will does not obtain grace by freedom, but obtains freedom by grace; when the feeling of delight has been imparted through the same grace, the human will is formed to endure; it is strengthened with unconquerable fortitude; controlled by grace, it never will perish, but, if grace forsake it, it will straightway fall; by the Lord's free mercy it is converted to good, and once converted it perseveres in good; the direction of the human will toward good, and after direction its continuation in good, depend solely upon God's will, not upon any merit of man. Thus there is left to man such free will, if we please so to call it, as he elsewhere describes: that except through grace the will can neither be converted to God nor abide in God; and whatever it can do it is able to do only through grace.

<table>
<tr><td>2.4</td><td align="center">How God Works in Men's Hearts</td></tr>
</table>

2.4.1–5   *(Man under Satan's control: but Scripture shows God making use of Satan in hardening the heart of the reprobate)*

2.4.6–8   *(God's providence overrules men's wills in external matters)*

2.4.6   *In actions of themselves neither good nor bad, we are not thrown on our own*

The force of God's providence extends to this point: not only that things occur as he foresees to be expedient, but that men's wills also incline to the same end. Indeed, if we ponder the direction of external things, we shall not doubt that to this extent they are left to human judgment. But if we lend our ears to the many testimonies which proclaim that the Lord also rules men's minds in external things, these will compel us to subordinate decision itself to the special impulse of God. Who inclined the wills of the Egyptians toward the Israelites so that they should lend them all their most precious vessels [Ex. 11:2–3]? They would never voluntarily have been so inclined. Therefore, their minds were more subject to the Lord than ruled by themselves.

2.4.8   *The question of "free will" does not depend on whether we can accomplish what we will, but whether we can will freely*

In discussing free will we are not asking whether a man is permitted to carry out and complete, despite external hindrances, whatever he has decided to do; but whether he has, in any respect whatever, both choice of judgment and inclination of will that are free.

2.5   Refutation of the Objections
                Commonly Put Forward in Defense of Free Will

2.5.1–5   *(Answers to arguments for free will alleged on grounds of common sense)*

FALLEN MAN OUGHT TO SEEK REDEMPTION IN CHRIST   2.6

(Through the Mediator, God is seen as a gracious Father)   2.6.1–2

Only the Mediator helps fallen man   2.6.1

The whole human race perished in the person of Adam. Consequently that original excellence and nobility which we have
recounted would be of no profit to us but would rather redound to
our greater shame, until God, who does not recognize as his handiwork men defiled and corrupted by sin, appeared as Redeemer in the
person of his only-begotten Son. Therefore, since we have fallen from
life into death, the whole knowledge of God the Creator that we have
discussed would be useless unless faith also followed, setting forth
for us God our Father in Christ. The natural order was that the frame
of the universe should be the school in which we were to learn piety,
and from it pass over to eternal life and perfect felicity. But after man's
rebellion, our eyes—wherever they turn—encounter God's curse.
This curse, while it seizes and envelops innocent creatures through
our fault, must overwhelm our souls with despair. For even if God
wills to manifest his fatherly favor to us in many ways, yet we cannot
by contemplating the universe infer that he is Father. Rather, conscience presses us within and shows in our sin just cause for his dis-
owning us and not regarding or recognizing us as his sons. Dullness
and ingratitude follow, for our minds, as they have been blinded, do
not perceive what is true. And as all our senses have become perverted, we wickedly defraud God of his glory.

Even the Old Covenant declared that there is no faith   2.6.2
in the gracious God apart from the Mediator

(Christ essential to the covenant and to true faith)   2.6.3–4

Faith in God is faith in Christ   2.6.4

I subscribe to the common saying that God is the object of faith, yet it
requires qualification. For Christ is not without reason called "the
image of the invisible God" [Col. 1:15]. This title warns us that, unless

God confronts us in Christ, we cannot come to know that we are saved. . . . [A]part from Christ the saving knowledge of God does not stand. From the beginning of the world he had consequently been set before all the elect that they should look unto him and put their trust in him.

In this sense Irenaeus writes that the Father, himself infinite, becomes finite in the Son, for he has accommodated himself to our little measure lest our minds be overwhelmed by the immensity of his glory. Fanatics, not reflecting upon this, twist a useful statement into an impious fantasy, as if there were in Christ only a portion of divinity, outflowing from the whole perfection of God. Actually, it means nothing else than that God is comprehended in Christ alone. John's saying has always been true: "He that does not have the Son does not have the Father" [I John 2:23 p.].

2.7   THE LAW WAS GIVEN, NOT TO RESTRAIN THE FOLK OF THE OLD COVENANT UNDER ITSELF, BUT TO FOSTER HOPE OF SALVATION IN CHRIST UNTIL HIS COMING

2.7.1–2   *(The moral and ceremonial law significant as leading to Christ)*

2.7.1   *The Mediator helps only fallen man*

The law was added about four hundred years after the death of Abraham [cf. Gal. 3:17]. From that continuing succession of witnesses which we have reviewed it may be gathered that this was not done to lead the chosen people away from Christ; but rather to hold their minds in readiness until his coming; even to kindle desire for him, and to strengthen their expectation, in order that they might not grow faint by too long delay. I understand by the word "law" not only the Ten Commandments, which set forth a godly and righteous rule of living, but the form of religion handed down by God through Moses. And Moses was not made a lawgiver to wipe out the blessing promised to the race of Abraham. Rather, we see him repeatedly reminding the Jews of that freely given covenant made with their fathers of which they were the heirs. It was as if he were sent to renew it.

2.7.3–5   *(We cannot fulfill the moral law)*

2.7.6–9   *(The law shows the righteousness of God, and as a mirror discloses our sinfulness, leading us to implore divine help)*

2.7.8   *The punitive function of the law in its work upon believers and unbelievers*

The wickedness and condemnation of us all are sealed by the testimony of the law. Yet this is not done to cause us to fall down in despair or, completely discouraged, to rush headlong over the brink—provided we duly profit by the testimony of the law. It is true that in this way the wicked are terrified, but because of their obstinacy of heart. For the children of God the knowledge of the law should have another purpose. The apostle testifies that we are indeed condemned by the judgment of the law, "so that every mouth may be stopped, and the whole world may be held accountable to God" [Rom. 3:19]. He teaches the same idea in yet another place: "For God has shut up all men in unbelief," not that he may destroy all or suffer all to perish, but "that he may have mercy upon all" [Rom. 11:32]. This means that, dismissing the stupid opinion of their own strength, they come to realize that they stand and are upheld by God's hand alone; that, naked and empty-handed, they flee to his mercy, repose entirely in it, hide deep within it, and seize upon it alone for righteousness and merit. For God's mercy is revealed in Christ to all who seek and wait upon it with true faith. In the precepts of the law, God is but the rewarder of perfect righteousness, which all of us lack, and conversely, the severe judge of evil deeds. But in Christ his face shines, full of grace and gentleness, even upon us poor and unworthy sinners.

(The law restrains malefactors and those who are not yet believers) 2.7.10–11

The law as protection of the community from unjust men 2.7.10

The second function of the law is this: at least by fear of punishment to restrain certain men who are untouched by any care for what is just and right unless compelled by hearing the dire threats in the law. But they are restrained, not because their inner mind is stirred or affected, but because, being bridled, so to speak, they keep their hands from outward activity, and hold inside the depravity that otherwise they would wantonly have indulged. Consequently, they are neither better nor more righteous before God.

(Principally it admonishes believers 2.7.12–13
and urges them on in well-doing)

Even the believers have need of the law 2.7.12

The third and principal use, which pertains more closely to the proper purpose of the law, finds its place among believers in whose hearts the Spirit of God already lives and reigns. For even though they have the law written and engraved upon their hearts by the finger of God [Jer. 31:33; Heb. 10:16], that is, have been so moved and quickened through the directing of the Spirit that they long to obey God, they still profit by the law in two ways.

Here is the best instrument for them to learn more thoroughly each day the nature of the Lord's will to which they aspire, and to confirm them in the understanding of it. . . .

Again, because we need not only teaching but also exhortation, the servant of God will also avail himself of this benefit of the law: by frequent meditation upon it to be aroused to obedience, be strengthened in it, and be drawn back from the slippery path of transgression.

2.7.14–17   *(Its so-called "abrogation" has reference to the liberation of the conscience, and the discontinuance of the ancient ceremonies)*

2.8   EXPLANATION OF THE MORAL LAW (THE TEN COMMANDMENTS)

2.8.1–2   *(The written moral law a statement of the natural law)*

2.8.3–5   *(We learn from it that God is our Father; that he is merciful and all-holy, and in kindness requires obedience)*

2.8.6–10   *(It is to be spiritually understood and interpreted with reference to the purpose of the Lawgiver)*

2.8.11–12   *(The two Tables of the Law, and the commandments rightly assigned to each)*

2.8.11   *The two Tables*

God has so divided his law into two parts, which contain the whole of righteousness, as to assign the first part to those duties of religion which particularly concern the worship of his majesty; the second, to the duties of love that have to do with men.

2.8.13–50   *(Detailed exposition of the individual commandments)*

2.8.17–21   *[Second Commandment: "You shall not make yourself a graven image, or any likeness of anything that is in heaven above, or in the earth beneath, or in the waters which are under the earth; you shall not adore or worship them." (Ex. 20:4–5, cf. Vg.)]*

2.8.22–27   *[Third Commandment: "You shall not take the name of Jehovah your God in vain." (Ex. 20:7)]*

[Fourth Commandment: "Remember to keep holy the Sabbath Day.   2.8.28–34
Six days you shall labor, and do all your work;
but the seventh day is a sabbath to Jehovah your God.
In it you shall not do any work," etc. (Ex. 20:8–10, cf. Vg.)]

[Fifth Commandment: "Honor your father and your mother   2.8.35–38
that you may be long-lived on the land
which Jehovah your God shall give you." (Ex. 20:12, cf. Vg.)]

[Sixth Commandment: "You shall not kill." (Ex. 20:13, Vg.)]   2.8.39–40

[Seventh Commandment: "You shall not commit adultery."   2.8.41–44
(Ex. 20:14, Vg.)]

[Eighth Commandment: "You shall not steal." (Ex. 20:15, Vg.)]   2.8.45–46

[Ninth Commandment: "You shall not be a false witness   2.8.47–48
against your neighbor." (Ex. 20:16)]

[Tenth Commandment: "You shall not covet   2.8.49–50
your neighbor's house," etc. (Ex. 20:17, Vg.)]

(Principles of the law in the light of Christ's teaching)   2.8.51–59

The sum of the law   2.8.51

Now it will not be difficult to decide the purpose of the whole law: the fulfillment of righteousness to form human life to the archetype of divine purity. For God has so depicted his character in the law that if any man carries out in deeds whatever is enjoined there, he will express the image of God, as it were, in his own life.

Love of neighbor   2.8.54

Here, therefore, let us stand fast: our life shall best conform to God's will and the prescription of the law when it is in every respect most fruitful for our brethren. . . . Hence it is very clear that we keep the commandments not by loving ourselves but by loving God and neighbor; that he lives the best and holiest life who lives and strives for himself as little as he can, and that no one lives in a worse or more evil manner than he who lives and strives for himself alone, and thinks about and seeks only his own advantage.

Who is our neighbor?   2.8.55

Now, since Christ has shown in the parable of the Samaritan that the term "neighbor" includes even the most remote person [Luke 10:36],

we are not expected to limit the precept of love to those in close relationships. . . . But I say: we ought to embrace the whole human race
without exception in a single feeling of love; here there is no distinction between barbarian and Greek, worthy and unworthy, friend and
enemy, since all should be contemplated in God, not in themselves.
When we turn aside from such contemplation, it is no wonder we
become entangled in many errors. Therefore, if we rightly direct our
love, we must first turn our eyes not to man, the sight of whom would
more often engender hate than love, but to God, who bids us extend
to all men the love we bear to him, that this may be an unchanging
principle: whatever the character of the man, we must yet love him
because we love God.

2.9   CHRIST, ALTHOUGH HE WAS KNOWN TO THE JEWS UNDER THE LAW,
WAS AT LENGTH CLEARLY REVEALED ONLY IN THE GOSPEL

2.9.1–2   *(The grace of Christ anticipated and manifested)*

2.9.3–5   *(Refutation of errors on the relation of law and gospel:*
intermediate position of John the Baptist)

2.10   *The Similarity of the Old and New Testaments*

2.10.1–6   *(The covenant in the Old Testament really the same as that of the New)*

2.10.2   *Chief points of agreement*

Both can be explained in one word. The covenant made with all
the patriarchs is so much like ours in substance and reality that the
two are actually one and the same. Yet they differ in the mode of
dispensation.

2.10.7–14   *(Argument concerning the hope of eternal life,*
showing that the Old Testament patriarchs
looked for fulfillment of the promises in the life to come)

2.10.15–22   *(This argument continued with references*
to passages from David, Job, Ezekiel, and others)

2.11   THE DIFFERENCE BETWEEN THE TWO TESTAMENTS

2.11.1–3—i.   *(The Old Testament differs from the New in five respects:*
representation of spiritual blessings by temporal)

CHRIST HAD TO BECOME MAN   2.12
IN ORDER TO FULFILL THE OFFICE OF MEDIATOR

Only he who was true God and true man   2.12.1
could bridge the gulf between God and ourselves

Now it was of the greatest importance for us that he who was to be
our Mediator be both true God and true man. If someone asks why
this is necessary, there has been no simple (to use the common expression) or absolute necessity. Rather, it has stemmed from a heavenly
decree, on which men's salvation depended. Our most merciful
Father decreed what was best for us. Since our iniquities, like a cloud
cast between us and him, had completely estranged us from the Kingdom of Heaven [cf. Isa. 59:2], no man, unless he belonged to God,
could serve as the intermediary to restore peace. But who might reach
to him? Any one of Adam's children? No, like their father, all of them
were terrified at the sight of God [Gen. 3:8]. One of the angels? They
also had need of a head, through whose bond they might cleave
firmly and undividedly to their God [cf. Eph. 1:22; Col. 2:10]. What
then? The situation would surely have been hopeless had the very
majesty of God not descended to us, since it was not in our power to
ascend to him. Hence, it was necessary for the Son of God to become
for us "Immanuel, that is, God with us" [Isa. 7:14; Matt. 1:23], and in
such a way that his divinity and our human nature might by mutual
connection grow together.

The Mediator must be true God and true man   2.12.2

What the Mediator was to accomplish was no common thing. His task was so to restore us to God's grace as to make of the children of men, children of God; of the heirs of Gehenna, heirs of the Heavenly Kingdom. Who could have done this had not the selfsame Son of God become the Son of man, and had not so taken what was ours as to impart what was his to us, and to make what was his by nature ours by grace? . . .

It was also imperative that he who was to become our Redeemer be true God and true man. It was his task to swallow up death. Who but the Life could do this? It was his task to conquer sin. Who but very Righteousness could do this? It was his task to rout the powers of world and air. Who but a power higher than world and air could do this? Now where does life or righteousness, or lordship and authority of heaven lie but with God alone? Therefore our most merciful God, when he willed that we be redeemed, made himself our Redeemer in the person of his only-begotten Son [cf. Rom. 5:8].

2.12.3   *Only he who was true God and true man*
could be obedient in our stead

The second requirement of our reconciliation with God was this: that man, who by his disobedience had become lost, should by way of remedy counter it with obedience, satisfy God's judgment, and pay the penalties for sin. Accordingly, our Lord came forth as true man and took the person and the name of Adam in order to take Adam's place in obeying the Father, to present our flesh as the price of satisfaction to God's righteous judgment, and, in the same flesh, to pay the penalty that we had deserved. . . .

Our common nature with Christ is the pledge of our fellowship with the Son of God; and clothed with our flesh he vanquished death and sin together that the victory and triumph might be ours. He offered as a sacrifice the flesh he received from us, that he might wipe out our guilt by his act of expiation and appease the Father's righteous wrath.

2.12.4–7   *(Objections to this doctrine answered)*

2.13   CHRIST ASSUMED THE TRUE SUBSTANCE OF HUMAN FLESH

2.13.1–2   *(Referring to ancient heresies, Calvin answers Menno Simons)*

2.13.3–4   *(The human descent and true humanity of Christ)*

2.13.4   *True man—and yet sinless! True man—and yet eternal God!*

And this remains for us an established fact: whenever Scripture calls our attention to the purity of Christ, it is to be understood of his true human nature, for it would have been superfluous to say that God is pure. Also, the sanctification of which John, ch. 17, speaks would have no place in divine nature [John 17:19]. Nor do we imagine that Adam's seed is twofold, even though no infection came to Christ. For the generation of man is not unclean and vicious of itself, but is so as an accidental quality arising from the Fall. No wonder, then, that Christ, through whom integrity was to be restored, was exempted from common corruption. They thrust upon us as something absurd the fact that if the Word of God became flesh, then he was confined within the narrow prison of an earthly body. This is mere impudence! For even if the Word in his immeasurable essence united with the nature of man into one person, we do not imagine that he was confined therein. Here is something marvelous: the Son of God descended from heaven in such a way that, without leaving heaven, he willed to be borne in the virgin's womb, to go about the earth, and to hang upon the cross; yet he continuously filled the world even as he had done from the beginning!

HOW THE TWO NATURES OF THE MEDIATOR MAKE ONE PERSON 2.14

(Explanation of the human and divine natures in Christ) 2.14.1–3

Duality and unity 2.14.1

We ought not to understand the statement that "the Word was made flesh" [John 1:14] in the sense that the Word was turned into flesh or confusedly mingled with flesh. Rather, it means that, because he chose for himself the virgin's womb as a temple in which to dwell, he who was the Son of God became the Son of man—not by confusion of substance, but by unity of person. For we affirm his divinity so joined and united with his humanity that each retains its distinctive nature unimpaired, and yet these two natures constitute one Christ.

If anything like this very great mystery can be found in human affairs, the most apposite parallel seems to be that of man, whom we see to consist of two substances. Yet neither is so mingled with the other as not to retain its own distinctive nature. For the soul is not the body, and the body is not the soul. Therefore, some things are said exclusively of the soul that can in no wise apply to the body; and of the body, again, that in no way fit the soul; of the whole man, that cannot refer—except inappropriately—to either soul or body separately. Finally, the characteristics of the mind are [sometimes] transferred to the body, and those of the body to the soul. Yet he who consists of these parts is one man, not many. Such expressions signify both that there is one person in man composed of two elements joined together, and that there are two diverse underlying natures that make up this person. Thus, also, the Scriptures speak of Christ: they sometimes attribute to him what must be referred solely to his humanity, sometimes what belongs uniquely to his divinity; and sometimes what embraces both natures but fits neither alone. And they so earnestly express this union of the two natures that is in Christ as sometimes to interchange them. This figure of speech is called by the ancient writers "the communicating of properties."

2.14.2 *Divinity and humanity in their relation to each other*

But the communicating of characteristics or properties consists in what Paul says: "God purchased the church with his blood" [Acts 20:28 p.], and "the Lord of glory was crucified" [I Cor. 2:8 p.]. John says the same: "The Word of life was handled" [I John 1:1 p.]. Surely God does not have blood, does not suffer, cannot be touched with hands. But since Christ, who was true God and also true man, was crucified and shed his blood for us, the things that he carried out in his human nature are transferred improperly, although not without reason, to his divinity. Here is a similar example: John teaches "that God laid down his life for us" [I John 3:16 p.]. Accordingly, there also a property of humanity is shared with the other nature. Again, when Christ, still living on earth, said: "No one has ascended into heaven but the Son of man who was in heaven" [John 3:13 p.], surely then, as man, in the flesh that he had taken upon himself, he was not in heaven. But because the selfsame one was both God and man, for the sake of the union of both natures he gave to the one what belonged to the other.

2.14.3 *The unity of the person of the Mediator*

But the passages that comprehend both natures at once, very many of which are to be found in John's Gospel, set forth his true substance most clearly of all. For one reads there neither of deity nor of humanity alone, but of both at once: he received from the Father the power of remitting sins [John 1:29], of raising to life whom he will, of bestowing righteousness, holiness, salvation; he was appointed judge of the living and the dead in order that he might be honored, even as the Father [John 5:21–23]. Lastly, he is called the "light of the world" [John 9:5; 8:12], the "good shepherd," the "only door" [John 10:11, 9], the "true vine" [John 15:1]. For the Son of God had been endowed with such prerogatives when he was manifested in the flesh. Even though along with the Father he held them before the creation of the world, it had not been in the same manner or respect, and they could not have been given to a man who was nothing but a man.

(Condemnation of the errors of Nestorius, Eutyches, and Servetus)   2.14.4–8

TO KNOW THE PURPOSE FOR WHICH CHRIST WAS SENT BY THE FATHER, AND WHAT HE CONFERRED UPON US, WE MUST LOOK ABOVE ALL AT THREE THINGS IN HIM: THE PROPHETIC OFFICE, KINGSHIP, AND PRIESTHOOD   2.15

(Christ's saving activity threefold: first the prophetic office)   2.15.1–2—i.

The need of understanding this doctrine: 2.15.1
Scriptural passages applicable to Christ's prophetic office

In order that faith may find a firm basis for salvation in Christ, and thus rest in him, this principle must be laid down: the office enjoined upon Christ by the Father consists of three parts. For he was given to be prophet, king, and priest. Yet it would be of little value to know these names without understanding their purpose and use.

The meaning of the prophetic office for us   2.15.2

Now it is to be noted that the title "Christ" pertains to these three offices: for we know that under the law prophets as well as priests and kings were anointed with holy oil. Hence the illustrious name of "Messiah" was also bestowed upon the promised Mediator. As I have elsewhere shown, I recognize that Christ was called Messiah especially with respect to, and by virtue of, his kingship. Yet his anointings as prophet and as priest have their place and must not be overlooked by us. Isaiah specifically mentions the former in these words: "The Spirit of the Lord Jehovah is upon me, because Jehovah has anointed me to preach to the humble, . . . to bring healing to the brokenhearted, to proclaim liberation to the captives . . . , to proclaim the year of the Lord's good pleasure," etc. [Isa. 61:1–2; cf. Luke 4:18]. We see that he was anointed by the Spirit to be herald and witness of the Father's grace. And that not in the common way—for he is distinguished from other teachers with a similar office. . . . This, however, remains certain: the perfect doctrine he has brought has made an end to all prophecies. . . . [T]he prophetic dignity in Christ leads us to know that in the sum of doctrine as he has given it to us all parts of perfect wisdom are contained.

(The kingly office—its spiritual character)

2.15.3 *The eternity of Christ's dominion*

I come now to kingship. It would be pointless to speak of this without first warning my readers that it is spiritual in nature. For from this
we infer its efficacy and benefit for us, as well as its whole force and
eternity. . . . [S]peaking in the person of God, David says: "Sit at my
right hand, till I make your enemies your footstool" [Ps. 110:1]. Here
he asserts that, no matter how many strong enemies plot to overthrow
the church, they do not have sufficient strength to prevail over God's
immutable decree by which he appointed his Son eternal King. Hence
it follows that the devil, with all the resources of the world, can never
destroy the church, founded as it is on the eternal throne of Christ.

Now with regard to the special application of this to each one of
us—the same "eternity" ought to inspire us to hope for blessed
immortality. For we see that whatever is earthly is of the world and of
time, and is indeed fleeting. Therefore Christ, to lift our hope to
heaven, declares that his "kingship is not of this world" [John 18:36].
In short, when any one of us hears that Christ's kingship is spiritual,
aroused by this word let him attain to the hope of a better life; and
since it is now protected by Christ's hand, let him await the full fruit
of this grace in the age to come.

2.15.4 *The blessing of Christ's kingly office for us*

We ought to know that the happiness promised us in Christ does not
consist in outward advantages—such as leading a joyous and peaceful life, having rich possessions, being safe from all harm, and
abounding with delights such as the flesh commonly longs after. No,
our happiness belongs to the heavenly life! . . . Christ enriches his
people with all things necessary for the eternal salvation of souls and
fortifies them with courage to stand unconquerable against all the
assaults of spiritual enemies. From this we infer that he rules—
inwardly and outwardly—more for our own sake than his. . . .

Thus it is that we may patiently pass through this life with its misery, hunger, cold, contempt, reproaches, and other troubles—content
with this one thing: that our King will never leave us destitute, but
will provide for our needs until, our warfare ended, we are called to
triumph. Such is the nature of his rule, that he shares with us all that
he has received from the Father. Now he arms and equips us with his
power, adorns us with his beauty and magnificence, enriches us with
his wealth. These benefits, then, give us the most fruitful occasion to
glory, and also provide us with confidence to struggle fearlessly

against the devil, sin, and death. Finally, clothed with his righteousness, we can valiantly rise above all the world's reproaches; and just as he himself freely lavishes his gifts upon us, so may we, in return, bring forth fruit to his glory.

The priestly office: reconciliation and intercession   2.15.6—iii.

Now we must speak briefly concerning the purpose and use of Christ's priestly office: as a pure and stainless Mediator he is by his holiness to reconcile us to God. But God's righteous curse bars our access to him, and God in his capacity as judge is angry toward us. Hence, an expiation must intervene in order that Christ as priest may obtain God's favor for us and appease his wrath. Thus Christ to perform this office had to come forward with a sacrifice. . . . The priestly office belongs to Christ alone because by the sacrifice of his death he blotted out our own guilt and made satisfaction for our sins [Heb. 9:22]. . . . [W]e or our prayers have no access to God unless Christ, as our High Priest, having washed away our sins, sanctifies us and obtains for us that grace from which the uncleanness of our transgressions and vices debars us. Thus we see that we must begin from the death of Christ in order that the efficacy and benefit of his priesthood may reach us.

It follows that he is an everlasting intercessor: through his pleading we obtain favor. Hence arises not only trust in prayer, but also peace for godly consciences, while they safely lean upon God's fatherly mercy and are surely persuaded that whatever has been consecrated through the Mediator is pleasing to God. Although God under the law commanded animal sacrifices to be offered to himself, in Christ there was a new and different order, in which the same one was to be both priest and sacrifice. This was because no other satisfaction adequate for our sins, and no man worthy to offer to God the only-begotten Son, could be found.

HOW CHRIST HAS FULFILLED THE FUNCTION OF REDEEMER   2.16
TO ACQUIRE SALVATION FOR US. HERE, ALSO, HIS DEATH AND
RESURRECTION ARE DISCUSSED, AS WELL AS HIS ASCENT INTO HEAVEN

(Alienated by sin from God, who yet loved us, we are reconciled by Christ)   2.16.1–4

The Redeemer   2.16.1

What we have said so far concerning Christ must be referred to this one objective: condemned, dead, and lost in ourselves, we should seek righteousness, liberation, life, and salvation in him. . . .

But here we must earnestly ponder how he accomplishes salvation for us.

2.16.2   *The awareness of God's wrath makes us thankful*
           for his loving act in Christ

But, before we go any farther, we must see in passing how fitting it was that God, who anticipates us by his mercy, should have been our enemy until he was reconciled to us through Christ. For how could he have given in his only-begotten Son a singular pledge of his love to us if he had not already embraced us with his free favor? . . .

Since our hearts cannot, in God's mercy, either seize upon life ardently enough or accept it with the gratefulness we owe, unless our minds are first struck and overwhelmed by fear of God's wrath and by dread of eternal death, we are taught by Scripture to perceive that apart from Christ, God is, so to speak, hostile to us, and his hand is armed for our destruction; to embrace his benevolence and fatherly love in Christ alone.

2.16.3   *God's wrath against unrighteousness;*
           his love precedes our reconciliation in Christ

For God, who is the highest righteousness, cannot love the unrighteousness that he sees in us all. All of us, therefore, have in ourselves something deserving of God's hatred. With regard to our corrupt nature and the wicked life that follows it, all of us surely displease God, are guilty in his sight, and are born to the damnation of hell. But because the Lord wills not to lose what is his in us, out of his own kindness he still finds something to love. However much we may be sinners by our own fault, we nevertheless remain his creatures. However much we have brought death upon ourselves, yet he has created us unto life. Thus he is moved by pure and freely given love of us to receive us into grace. Since there is a perpetual and irreconcilable disagreement between righteousness and unrighteousness, so long as we remain sinners he cannot receive us completely. Therefore, to take away all cause for enmity and to reconcile us utterly to himself, he wipes out all evil in us by the expiation set forth in the death of Christ; that we, who were previously unclean and impure, may show ourselves righteous and holy in his sight. Therefore, by his love God the Father goes before and anticipates our reconciliation in Christ. Indeed, "because he first loved us" [I John 4:19], he afterward reconciles us to himself. But until Christ succors us by his death, the unrighteousness that deserves God's indignation remains in us, and is accursed and condemned before him. Hence, we can be fully and firmly joined with God only when Christ joins us with him. If, then, we would be assured that God is pleased with and kindly disposed toward us, we must fix our eyes and minds on Christ alone. For actually, through him alone we escape the imputation of our sins to us— an imputation bringing with it the wrath of God.

The work of atonement derives from God's love;   2.16.4
therefore it has not established the latter

For this reason, Paul says that the love with which God embraced us "before the creation of the world" was established and grounded in Christ [Eph. 1:4–5]. These things are plain and in agreement with Scripture, and beautifully harmonize those passages in which it is said that God declared his love toward us in giving his only-begotten Son to die [John 3:16]; and, conversely, that God was our enemy before he was again made favorable to us by Christ's death [Rom. 5:10].

(The effects of the obedience and death of Christ)   2.16.5–7

Christ has redeemed us through his obedience,   2.16.5
which he practiced throughout his life

Now someone asks, How has Christ abolished sin, banished the separation between us and God, and acquired righteousness to render God favorable and kindly toward us? To this we can in general reply that he has achieved this for us by the whole course of his obedience. This is proved by Paul's testimony: "As by one man's disobedience many were made sinners, so by one man's obedience we are made righteous" [Rom. 5:19 p.]. . . . In short, from the time when he took on the form of a servant, he began to pay the price of liberation in order to redeem us. . . .

(The condemnation through Pilate)

This is our acquittal: the guilt that held us liable for punishment has been transferred to the head of the Son of God [Isa. 53:12]. We must, above all, remember this substitution, lest we tremble and remain anxious throughout life—as if God's righteous vengeance, which the Son of God has taken upon himself, still hung over us.

"Crucified"   2.16.6

The form of Christ's death also embodies a singular mystery. The cross was accursed, not only in human opinion but by decree of God's law [Deut. 21:23]. Hence, when Christ is hanged upon the cross, he makes himself subject to the curse. . . . The apostle testifies this more openly when he teaches: "For our sake he who knew no sin was made sin by the Father, so that in him we might be made the righteousness of God" [II Cor. 5:21]. The Son of God, utterly clean of all fault, nevertheless took upon himself the shame and reproach of our iniquities, and in return clothed us with his purity. It seems that Paul meant the same thing when he says of sin, "He condemned sin in his flesh" [Rom. 8:3 p.]. The Father destroyed the force of sin when the curse of sin was transferred to Christ's flesh. There, then, is the meaning of this saying: Christ was offered to the Father in death as an expiatory sacrifice that when he discharged all satisfaction through his sacrifice, we might cease to be afraid of God's wrath.

2.16.7   *"Dead and buried"*

There follows in the Creed: "He was dead and buried." Here again is to be seen how he in every respect took our place to pay the price of our redemption. Death held us captive under its yoke; Christ, in our stead, gave himself over to its power to deliver us from it. So the apostle understands it when he writes: "He tasted death for everyone" [Heb. 2:9 p.]. By dying, he ensured that we would not die, or—which is the same thing—redeemed us to life by his own death. . . . [H]is purpose was "that through death he might destroy him who had the power of death, that is, the devil, and deliver all those who through fear of death were subject to lifelong bondage" [Heb. 2:14–15]. This is the first fruit that his death brought to us.

The second effect of Christ's death upon us is this: by our participation in it, his death mortifies our earthly members so that they may no longer perform their functions; and it kills the old man in us that he may not flourish and bear fruit. Christ's burial has the same effect: we ourselves as partakers in it are buried with him to sin.

2.16.8–12   *(Explanation of the doctrine of the descent into hell)*

2.16.10   *The "descent into hell" as an expression*
of the spiritual torment that Christ underwent for us

The point is that the Creed sets forth what Christ suffered in the sight of men, and then appositely speaks of that invisible and incomprehensible judgment which he underwent in the sight of God in order that we might know not only that Christ's body was given as the price of our redemption, but that he paid a greater and more excellent price in suffering in his soul the terrible torments of a condemned and forsaken man.

(Christ's resurrection, ascension, and heavenly session)   2.16.13–16

"On the third day he rose again from the dead"   2.16.13

Next comes the resurrection from the dead. Without this what we have said so far would be incomplete. For since only weakness appears in the cross, death, and burial of Christ, faith must leap over all these things to attain its full strength. We have in his death the complete fulfillment of salvation, for through it we are reconciled to God, his righteous judgment is satisfied, the curse is removed, and the penalty paid in full. Nevertheless, we are said to "have been born anew to a living hope" not through his death but "through his resurrection" [I Pet. 1:3 p.]. For as he, in rising again, came forth victor over death, so the victory of our faith over death lies in his resurrection alone. . . . Therefore, we divide the substance of our salvation between Christ's death and resurrection as follows: through his death, sin was wiped out and death extinguished; through his resurrection, righteousness was restored and life raised up, so that— thanks to his resurrection—his death manifested its power and efficacy in us. . . .

So then, let us remember that whenever mention is made of his death alone, we are to understand at the same time what belongs to his resurrection. Also, the same synecdoche applies to the word "resurrection": whenever it is mentioned separately from death, we are to understand it as including what has to do especially with his death. But because by rising again he obtained the victor's prize—that there might be resurrection and life.

"Ascended into heaven"   2.16.14

To the resurrection is quite appropriately joined the ascent into heaven. Now having laid aside the mean and lowly state of mortal life and the shame of the cross, Christ by rising again began to show forth his glory and power more fully. Yet he truly inaugurated his Kingdom only at his ascension into heaven. The apostle shows this when he teaches that Christ "ascended . . . that he might fill all things" [Eph. 4:10, cf. Vg.].

"Seated at the right hand of the Father"   2.16.15

So it was said that Christ, in whom the Father wills to be exalted and through whose hand he wills to reign, was received at God's right hand. This is as if it were said that Christ was invested with lordship over heaven and earth, and solemnly entered into possession of the government committed to him—and that he not only entered into possession once for all, but continues in it, until he shall come down on Judgment Day.

2.16.16   *Benefits imparted to our faith by Christ's ascension*

From this our faith receives many benefits. First it understands that the Lord by his ascent to heaven opened the way into the Heavenly Kingdom, which had been closed through Adam [John 14:3] . . .

Secondly, as faith recognizes, it is to our great benefit that Christ resides with the Father. For, having entered a sanctuary not made with hands, he appears before the Father's face as our constant advocate and intercessor [Heb. 7:25; 9:11–12; Rom. 8:34]. Thus he turns the Father's eyes to his own righteousness to avert his gaze from our sins. He so reconciles the Father's heart to us that by his intercession he prepares a way and access for us to the Father's throne. He fills with grace and kindness the throne that for miserable sinners would otherwise have been filled with dread.

Thirdly, faith comprehends his might, in which reposes our strength, power, wealth, and glorying against hell. "When he ascended into heaven he led a captivity captive" [Eph. 4:8, cf. Vg.; cf. Ps. 68:18], and despoiling his enemies, he enriched his own people, and daily lavishes spiritual riches upon them.

2.16.17   *"From whence he shall come to judge the living and the dead"*

Christ gives to his own people clear testimonies of his very present power. Yet his Kingdom lies hidden in the earth, so to speak, under the lowness of the flesh. It is right, therefore, that faith be called to ponder that visible presence of Christ which he will manifest on the Last Day. For he will come down from heaven in the same visible form in which he was seen to ascend [Acts 1:11; Matt. 24:30]. And he will appear to all with the ineffable majesty of his Kingdom, with the glow of immortality, with the boundless power of divinity, with a guard of angels. From thence we are commanded to await him as our Redeemer on that day when he will separate the lambs from the goats, the elect from the reprobate [Matt. 25:31–33]. No one—living or dead—shall escape his judgment. The sound of the trumpet will be heard from the ends of the earth, and by it all will be summoned before his judgment seat, both those still alive at that day and those whom death had previously taken from the company of the living [I Thess. 4:16–17].

(Concluding remarks on the Apostles' Creed   2.16.18–19
and the sufficiency of Christ)

The Judge is the—Redeemer!   2.16.18

Hence arises a wonderful consolation: that we perceive judgment to
be in the hands of him who has already destined us to share with him
the honor of judging [cf. Matt. 19:28]! Far indeed is he from mounting
his judgment seat to condemn us! How could our most merciful Ruler
destroy his people? How could the Head scatter his own members?
How could our Advocate condemn his clients? For if the apostle dares
exclaim that with Christ interceding for us there is no one who can
come forth to condemn us [Rom. 8:34, 33], it is much more true, then,
that Christ as Intercessor will not condemn those whom he has received
into his charge and protection. No mean assurance, this—that we
shall be brought before no other judgment seat than that of our
Redeemer, to whom we must look for our salvation! Moreover, he who
now promises eternal blessedness through the gospel will then fulfill
his promise in judgment. Therefore, by giving all judgment to the Son
[John 5:22], the Father has honored him to the end that he may care
for the consciences of his people, who tremble in dread of judgment.

Christ alone in all the clauses of the Creed   2.16.19

We see that our whole salvation and all its parts are comprehended in
Christ [Acts 4:12]. We should therefore take care not to derive the least
portion of it from anywhere else. . . . In short, since rich store of every
kind of good abounds in him, let us drink our fill from this fountain,
and from no other.

CHRIST RIGHTLY AND PROPERLY SAID TO HAVE MERITED   2.17
GOD'S GRACE AND SALVATION FOR US

Christ's merit does not exclude God's free grace, but precedes it   2.17.1

Inasmuch as Christ's merit depends upon God's grace alone, which
has ordained this manner of salvation for us, it is just as properly
opposed to all human righteousness as God's grace is.

Scripture couples God's grace and Christ's merit   2.17.2

The merit of Christ in the witness of Scripture   2.17.3

The substitution of Christ   2.17.4

2.17.5 *Christ's death the price of our redemption*

2.17.6 *Christ acquired no merit for himself*

Book III

The Way in Which We Receive the Grace of Christ: What Benefits Come to Us from It, and What Effects Follow

The Holy Spirit as the bond that unites us to Christ   3.1.1

We must now examine this question. How do we receive those benefits which the Father bestowed on his only-begotten Son—not for Christ's own private use, but that he might enrich poor and needy men? First, we must understand that as long as Christ remains outside of us, and we are separated from him, all that he has suffered and done for the salvation of the human race remains useless and of no value for us. Therefore, to share with us what he has received from the Father, he had to become ours and to dwell within us. . . . [W]e obtain this by faith. Yet since we see that not all indiscriminately embrace that communion with Christ which is offered through the gospel, reason itself teaches us to climb higher and to examine into the secret energy of the Spirit, by which we come to enjoy Christ and all his benefits. . . .

There is good reason for the repeated mention of the "testimony of the Spirit," a testimony we feel engraved like a seal upon our hearts, with the result that it seals the cleansing and sacrifice of Christ. . . . [T]he Holy Spirit is the bond by which Christ effectually unites us to himself.

3.1.2   *How and why Christ was endowed with the Holy Spirit*

But, in order to get a clearer notion of this matter, so well worth investigating, we must bear in mind that Christ came endowed with the Holy Spirit in a special way: that is, to separate us from the world and to gather us unto the hope of the eternal inheritance. Hence he is called the "Spirit of sanctification" [cf. II Thess. 2:13; I Pet. 1:2; Rom. 1:4] because he not only quickens and nourishes us by a general power that is visible both in the human race and in the rest of the living creatures, but he is also the root and seed of heavenly life in us. . . . God the Father gives us the Holy Spirit for his Son's sake, and yet has bestowed the whole fullness of the Spirit upon the Son to be minister and steward of his liberality. For this reason, the Spirit is sometimes called the "Spirit of the Father," sometimes the "Spirit of the Son."

3.1.3   *Titles of the Holy Spirit in Scripture*

3.1.4   *Faith as the work of the Spirit*

But faith is the principal work of the Holy Spirit. Consequently, the terms commonly employed to express his power and working are, in large measure, referred to it because by faith alone he leads us into the light of the gospel. . . . Paul shows the Spirit to be the inner teacher by whose effort the promise of salvation penetrates into our minds, a promise that would otherwise only strike the air or beat upon our ears. . . . Consequently, he may rightly be called the key that unlocks for us the treasures of the Kingdom of Heaven [cf. Rev. 3:7]; and his illumination, the keenness of our insight.

3.2   FAITH: ITS DEFINITION SET FORTH, AND ITS PROPERTIES EXPLAINED

3.2.1   *The object of faith is Christ*

But it will be easy to understand all these matters after a clearer definition of faith has been presented, to enable our readers to grasp its force and nature. We may well recall here what was explained before: First, God lays down for us through the law what we should do; if we then fail in any part of it, that dreadful sentence of eternal death which it pronounces will rest upon us. Secondly, it is not only hard, but above our strength and beyond all our abilities, to fulfill the law to the letter; thus, if we look to ourselves only, and ponder what condition we deserve, no trace of good hope will remain; but cast away by God, we shall lie under eternal death. Thirdly, it has been explained that there is but one means of liberation that can rescue us from such miserable calamity: the appearance of Christ the Redeemer, through whose hand the Heavenly Father, pitying us out of his infinite goodness and mercy, willed to help us; if, indeed, with firm faith we embrace this mercy and rest in it with steadfast hope.

(Faith involves knowledge; the true doctrine obscured by the Scholastic notion of implicit faith) 3.2.2–5

Faith rests upon knowledge, not upon pious ignorance 3.2.2

Faith rests not on ignorance, but on knowledge. And this is, indeed, knowledge not only of God but of the divine will. We do not obtain salvation either because we are prepared to embrace as true whatever the church has prescribed, or because we turn over to it the task of inquiring and knowing. But we do so when we know that God is our merciful Father, because of reconciliation effected through Christ [II Cor. 5:18–19], and that Christ has been given to us as righteousness, sanctification, and life. By this knowledge, I say, not by submission of our feeling, do we obtain entry into the Kingdom of Heaven.

(Relation of faith to the Word and brief definition of faith) 3.2.6–7

Faith rests upon God's Word 3.2.6

This, then, is the true knowledge of Christ, if we receive him as he is offered by the Father: namely, clothed with his gospel. For just as he has been appointed as the goal of our faith, so we cannot take the right road to him unless the gospel goes before us. And there, surely, the treasures of grace are opened to us; for if they had been closed, Christ would have benefited us little. . . .

Therefore if faith turns away even in the slightest degree from this goal toward which it should aim, it does not keep its own nature, but becomes uncertain credulity and vague error of mind. The same Word is the basis whereby faith is supported and sustained; if it turns away from the Word, it falls. Therefore, take away the Word and no faith will then remain. . . .

Now, therefore, we hold faith to be a knowledge of God's will toward us, perceived from his Word. But the foundation of this is a preconceived conviction of God's truth. As for its certainty, so long as your mind is at war with itself, the Word will be of doubtful and weak authority, or rather of none. And it is not even enough to believe that God is trustworthy [cf. Rom. 3:3], who can neither deceive nor lie [cf. Titus 1:2], unless you hold to be beyond doubt that whatever proceeds from him is sacred and inviolable truth.

3.2.7   *Faith arises from God's promise of grace in Christ*

But since man's heart is not aroused to faith at every word of God, we must find out at this point what, strictly speaking, faith looks to in the Word. . . .

Now we shall possess a right definition of faith if we call it a firm and certain knowledge of God's benevolence toward us, founded upon the truth of the freely given promise in Christ, both revealed to our minds and sealed upon our hearts through the Holy Spirit.

3.2.8–13 *(Various unacceptable significations of the term "faith")*

3.2.8   *"Formed" and "unformed" faith*

Since faith embraces Christ, as offered to us by the Father [cf. John 6:29]—that is, since he is offered not only for righteousness, forgiveness of sins, and peace, but also for sanctification [cf. I Cor. 1:30] and the fountain of the water of life [John 7:38; cf. 4:14]—without a doubt, no one can duly know him without at the same time apprehending the sanctification of the Spirit. Or, if anyone desires some plainer statement, faith rests upon the knowledge of Christ. And Christ cannot be known apart from the sanctification of his Spirit. It follows that faith can in no wise be separated from a devout disposition.

3.2.14–15 *(Detailed examination of what the definition of faith*
in paragraph 7 implies: the element of knowledge)

3.2.14   *Faith as higher knowledge*

When we call faith "knowledge" we do not mean comprehension of the sort that is commonly concerned with those things which fall under human sense perception. For faith is so far above sense that man's mind has to go beyond and rise above itself in order to attain it. Even where the mind has attained, it does not comprehend what it feels. But while it is persuaded of what it does not grasp, by the very certainty of its persuasion it understands more than if it perceived anything human by its own capacity. . . . [F]aith is frequently called "recognition" [see Eph. 1:17; 4:13; Col. 1:9; 3:10; I Tim. 2:4; Titus 1:1; Philemon 6; II Peter 2:21], but by John, "knowledge." For he declares that believers know themselves to be God's children [I John 3:2]. And obviously they surely know this. But they are more strengthened by the persuasion of divine truth than instructed by rational proof. Paul's words also point this out: "While dwelling in this body, we wander from the Lord, for we walk by faith, not by sight" [II Cor. 5:6–7].

By these words he shows that those things which we know through faith are nonetheless absent from us and go unseen. From this we conclude that the knowledge of faith consists in assurance rather than in comprehension.

Faith implies certainty

3.2.15

We add the words "sure and firm" in order to express a more solid constancy of persuasion. For, as faith is not content with a doubtful and changeable opinion, so is it not content with an obscure and confused conception; but requires full and fixed certainty, such as men are wont to have from things experienced and proved. For unbelief is so deeply rooted in our hearts, and we are so inclined to it, that not without hard struggle is each one able to persuade himself of what all confess with the mouth: namely, that God is faithful. . . .

The apostle derives confidence from faith, and from confidence, in turn, boldness. For he states: "Through Christ we have boldness and access with confidence which is through faith in him" [Eph. 3:12 p., cf. Vg.]. By these words he obviously shows that there is no right faith except when we dare with tranquil hearts to stand in God's sight. This boldness arises only out of a sure confidence in divine benevolence and salvation. This is so true that the word "faith" is very often used for confidence.

(Certainty of faith in relation to fear)

3.2.16–28

Certainty of faith

3.2.16

Here, indeed, is the chief hinge on which faith turns: that we do not regard the promises of mercy that God offers as true only outside ourselves, but not at all in us; rather that we make them ours by inwardly embracing them. . . . Briefly, he alone is truly a believer who, convinced by a firm conviction that God is a kindly and well-disposed Father toward him, promises himself all things on the basis of his generosity; who, relying upon the promises of divine benevolence toward him, lays hold on an undoubted expectation of salvation.

Faith in the struggle against temptation

3.2.17

Surely, while we teach that faith ought to be certain and assured, we cannot imagine any certainty that is not tinged with doubt, or any assurance that is not assailed by some anxiety. On the other hand, we say that believers are in perpetual conflict with their own unbelief. Far, indeed, are we from putting their consciences in any peaceful repose, undisturbed by any tumult at all. Yet, once again, we deny that, in whatever way they are afflicted, they fall away and depart from the certain assurance received from God's mercy.

3.2.18 *The conflict in the heart of the believer*

But if in the believing mind certainty is mixed with doubt, do we not always come back to this, that faith does not rest in a certain and clear knowledge, but only in an obscure and confused knowledge of the divine will toward us? Not at all. For even if we are distracted by various thoughts, we are not on that account completely divorced from faith. Nor if we are troubled on all sides by the agitation of unbelief, are we for that reason immersed in its abyss. If we are struck, we are not for that reason cast down from our position. For the end of the conflict is always this: that faith ultimately triumphs over those difficulties which besiege and seem to imperil it.

3.2.19 *Even weak faith is real faith*

Bound with the fetters of an earthly body, however much we are shadowed on every side with great darkness, we are nevertheless illumined as much as need be for firm assurance when, to show forth his mercy, the light of God sheds even a little of its radiance.

3.2.20 *The weakness and strength of faith*

Whether adversities reveal God's wrath, or the conscience finds in itself the proof and ground thereof, thence unbelief obtains weapons and devices to overthrow faith. Yet these are always directed to this objective: that, thinking God to be against us and hostile to us, we should not hope for any help from him, and should fear him as if he were our deadly enemy.

3.2.21 *The Word of God as the shield of faith*

To bear these attacks faith arms and fortifies itself with the Word of the Lord. And when any sort of temptation assails us—suggesting that God is our enemy because he is unfavorable toward us—faith, on the other hand, replies that while he afflicts us he is also merciful because his chastisement arises out of love rather than wrath. When one is stricken by the thought that God is Avenger of iniquities, faith sets over against this the fact that his pardon is ready for all iniquities whenever the sinner betakes himself to the Lord's mercy. Thus the godly mind, however strange the ways in which it is vexed and troubled, finally surmounts all difficulties, and never allows itself to be deprived of assurance of divine mercy.

"Fear and trembling"   3.2.23

Nothing prevents believers from being afraid and at the same time possessing the surest consolation; according as they turn their eyes now upon their own vanity, and then bring the thought of their minds to bear upon the truth of God.

The indestructible certainty of faith rests upon Christ's oneness with us   3.2.24

Therefore unbelief and good hope must alternately reign in your mind. As if we ought to think of Christ, standing afar off and not rather dwelling in us! For we await salvation from him not because he appears to us afar off, but because he makes us, ingrafted into his body, participants not only in all his benefits but also in himself. So I turn this argument of theirs back against them: if you contemplate yourself, that is sure damnation. But since Christ has been so imparted to you with all his benefits that all his things are made yours, that you are made a member of him, indeed one with him, his righteousness overwhelms your sins; his salvation wipes out your condemnation; with his worthiness he intercedes that your unworthiness may not come before God's sight. Surely this is so: We ought not to separate Christ from ourselves or ourselves from him. Rather we ought to hold fast bravely with both hands to that fellowship by which he has bound himself to us. . . . [T]hat condemnation which we of ourselves deserve has been swallowed up by the salvation that is in Christ. . . . Christ is not outside us but dwells within us. Not only does he cleave to us by an indivisible bond of fellowship, but with a wonderful communion, day by day, he grows more and more into one body with us, until he becomes completely one with us.

Faith assures us not of earthly prosperity but of God's favor   3.2.28

Now, in the divine benevolence, which faith is said to look to, we understand the possession of salvation and eternal life is obtained. For if, while God is favorable, no good can be lacking, when he assures us of his love we are abundantly and sufficiently assured of salvation. . . . "Let him show his face," says the prophet, "and we will be saved" [Ps. 80:3 p.; cf. Ps. 79:4, Vg.]. Hence Scripture establishes this as the sum of our salvation, that he has abolished all enmities and received us into grace [Eph. 2:14]. . . . For faith does not certainly promise itself either length of years or honor or riches in this life, since the Lord willed that none of these things be appointed for us. But it is content with this certainty: that, however many things fail us that have to do with the maintenance of this life, God will never fail. Rather, the chief assurance of faith rests in the expectation of the life to come, which has been placed beyond doubt through the Word of God. Yet whatever earthly miseries and calamities await those whom God has embraced in his love, these cannot hinder his benevolence from being their full happiness. Accordingly, when we would express the sum of blessedness, we have mentioned the grace of God; for from this fountain every sort of good thing flows unto us. . . .

3.2.29–32   *(Basis of faith the free promise, given in the Word, of grace in Christ)*

3.2.29   *God's promise the support of faith*

We make the freely given promise of God the foundation of faith because upon it faith properly rests. Faith is certain that God is true in all things whether he command or forbid, whether he promise or threaten; and it also obediently receives his commandments, observes his prohibitions, heeds his threats. Nevertheless, faith properly begins with the promise, rests in it, and ends in it. For in God faith seeks life: a life that is not found in commandments or declarations of penalties, but in the promise of mercy, and only in a freely given promise. For a conditional promise that sends us back to our own works does not promise life unless we discern its presence in ourselves. Therefore, if we would not have our faith tremble and waver, we must buttress it with the promise of salvation, which is willingly and freely offered to us by the Lord in consideration of our misery rather than our deserts. . . .

When we say that faith must rest upon a freely given promise, we do not deny that believers embrace and grasp the Word of God in every respect: but we point out the promise of mercy as the proper goal of faith.

3.2.30   *Why faith depends solely on the promise of grace*

It is our intention to make only these two points: first, that faith does not stand firm until a man attains to the freely given promise; second, that it does not reconcile us to God at all unless it joins us to Christ.

3.2.32   *The promise of faith fulfilled in Christ*

It is not without cause that we include all the promises in Christ, since the apostle includes the whole gospel under the knowledge of him [cf. Rom. 1:17], and elsewhere teaches that "however many are the promises of God, in him they find their yea and amen" [II Cor. 1:20 p.]. The reason for this fact is at hand; for if God promises anything, by it he witnesses his benevolence, so that there is no promise of his which is not a testimony of his love. . . .

But it is indisputable that no one is loved by God apart from Christ.

(Faith revealed in our hearts by the Spirit) 3.2.33–37

The Word becomes efficacious for our faith through the Holy Spirit 3.2.33

And this bare and external proof of the Word of God should have been amply sufficient to engender faith, did not our blindness and perversity prevent it. But our mind has such an inclination to vanity that it can never cleave fast to the truth of God; and it has such a dullness that it is always blind to the light of God's truth. Accordingly, without the illumination of the Holy Spirit, the Word can do nothing. From this, also, it is clear that faith is much higher than human understanding. And it will not be enough for the mind to be illumined by the Spirit of God unless the heart is also strengthened and supported by his power. In this matter the Schoolmen go completely astray, who in considering faith identify it with a bare and simple assent arising out of knowledge, and leave out confidence and assurance of heart. In both ways, therefore, faith is a singular gift of God, both in that the mind of man is purged so as to be able to taste the truth of God and in that his heart is established therein. For the Spirit is not only the initiator of faith, but increases it by degrees, until by it he leads us to the Kingdom of Heaven.

Only the Holy Spirit leads us to Christ 3.2.34

As we cannot come to Christ unless we be drawn by the Spirit of God, so when we are drawn we are lifted up in mind and heart above our understanding. For the soul, illumined by him, takes on a new keenness, as it were, to contemplate the heavenly mysteries, whose splendor had previously blinded it. And man's understanding, thus beamed by the light of the Holy Spirit, then at last truly begins to taste those things which belong to the Kingdom of God, having formerly been quite foolish and dull in tasting them. . . . Indeed, the Word of God is like the sun, shining upon all those to whom it is proclaimed, but with no effect among the blind. Now, all of us are blind by nature in this respect. Accordingly, it cannot penetrate into our minds unless the Spirit, as the inner teacher, through his illumination makes entry for it.

3.2.35   *Without the Spirit man is incapable of faith*

Paul calls faith itself, which the Spirit gives us but which we do not
have by nature, "the spirit of faith" [II Cor. 4:13]. He therefore prays
that in the Thessalonians "God . . . may fulfill with power all his good
pleasure . . . and work of faith" [II Thess. 1:11, cf. Vg.]. Here Paul calls
faith "the work of God," and instead of distinguishing it by an adjec-
tive, appropriately calls it "good pleasure." Thus he denies that man
himself initiates faith, and not satisfied with this, he adds that it is a
manifestation of God's power. . . . To sum up: Christ, when he illumines us into faith by the power of his Spirit, at the same time so
engrafts us into his body that we become partakers of every good.

3.2.36   *Faith as a matter of the heart*

It now remains to pour into the heart itself what the mind has
absorbed. For the Word of God is not received by faith if it flits about
in the top of the brain, but when it takes root in the depth of the heart
that it may be an invincible defense to withstand and drive off all the
stratagems of temptation. . . . But if it is true that the mind's real
understanding is illumination by the Spirit of God, then in such confirmation of the heart his power is much more clearly manifested, to
the extent that the heart's distrust is greater than the mind's blindness. It is harder for the heart to be furnished with assurance than for
the mind to be endowed with thought. The Spirit accordingly serves
as a seal, to seal up in our hearts those very promises the certainty of
which it has previously impressed upon our minds; and takes the
place of a guarantee to confirm and establish them.

3.2.38–40   *(Refutation of Scholastic objections to this)*

3.2.41–43   *(Relation of faith to hope and love)*

3.2.42   *Faith and hope belong together*

Wherever this faith is alive, it must have along with it the hope of
eternal salvation as its inseparable companion. Or rather, it engenders
and brings forth hope from itself. . . . [I]f faith . . . is a sure persuasion
of the truth of God—that it can neither lie to us, nor deceive us, nor
become void—then those who have grasped this certainty assuredly
expect the time to come when God will fulfill his promises, which
they are persuaded cannot but be true. Accordingly, in brief, hope is
nothing else than the expectation of those things which faith has
believed to have been truly promised by God. Thus, faith believes

God to be true, hope awaits the time when his truth shall be manifested; faith believes that he is our Father, hope anticipates that he will
ever show himself to be a Father toward us; faith believes that eternal
life has been given to us, hope anticipates that it will some time be
revealed; faith is the foundation upon which hope rests, hope nourishes and sustains faith. For as no one except him who already
believes His promises can look for anything from God, so again the
weakness of our faith must be sustained and nourished by patient
hope and expectation, lest it fail and grow faint. For this reason, Paul
rightly sets our salvation in hope [Rom. 8:24]. For hope, while it
awaits the Lord in silence, restrains faith that it may not fall headlong
from too much haste. Hope strengthens faith, that it may not waver in
God's promises, or begin to doubt concerning their truth. Hope
refreshes faith, that it may not become weary. It sustains faith to the
final goal, that it may not fail in mid-course, or even at the starting
gate. In short, by unremitting renewing and restoring, it invigorates
faith again and again with perseverance.

And we shall better see in how many ways the support of hope is
necessary to establish faith if we ponder how many forms of temptation assail and strike those who have embraced the Word of God.
First, the Lord by deferring his promises often holds our minds in suspense longer than we would wish. Here it is the function of hope to
carry out what the prophet bids: "That, if they should tarry, we wait
for them" [Hab. 2:3 p.]. Occasionally he not only allows us to faint but
exhibits open indignation toward us. Here it is much more necessary
for hope to help us, that, according to another prophet's statement,
we may "wait for the Lord who hid his face from . . . Jacob" [Isa. 8:17].
Scoffers also rise up, as Peter says [II Pet. 3:3], asking: "Where is the
promise of his coming? Since the fathers fell asleep, all things continue as they were from the beginning of creation" [II Pet. 3:4, Vg.].
Indeed, the flesh and the world whisper these same things to us. Here
we must keep our faith buttressed by patient hope, so fixed upon the
contemplation of eternity as to reckon a thousand years as one day
[Ps. 90:4; II Pet. 3:8].

Faith and hope have the same foundation: God's mercy   3.2.43

Hope is nothing but the nourishment and strength of faith.

Sometimes they are joined together, as in the same letter: "So that
your faith and hope are in God" [I Pet. 1:21]. But in the letter to the
Philippians, Paul derives expectation from hope because by hoping
patiently we suspend our own desires until God's appointed time
is revealed [Phil. 1:20]. . . . [E]mbracing the testimony of the gospel

concerning freely given love, we look for the time when God will openly show that which is now hidden under hope. . . .

Hope can have no other goal than faith has. But we have already explained very clearly that the single goal of faith is the mercy of God—to which it ought, so to speak, to look with both eyes.

| 3.3 | OUR REGENERATION BY FAITH: REPENTANCE |

3.3.1–4   *(Repentance the fruit of faith:*
review of some errors connected with this point)

3.3.1   *Repentance as a consequence of faith*

Even though we have taught in part how faith possesses Christ, and how through it we enjoy his benefits, this would still remain obscure if we did not add an explanation of the effects we feel. With good reason, the sum of the gospel is held to consist in repentance and forgiveness of sins [Luke 24:47; Acts 5:31]. Any discussion of faith, therefore, that omitted these two topics would be barren and mutilated and well-nigh useless. Now, both repentance and forgiveness of sins—that is, newness of life and free reconciliation—are conferred on us by Christ, and both are attained by us through faith.

3.3.2   *Repentance has its foundation in the gospel, which faith embraces*

While Christ the Lord and John preach in this manner: "Repent, for the Kingdom of Heaven is at hand" [Matt. 3:2], do they not derive the reason for repenting from grace itself and the promise of salvation? Accordingly, therefore, their words mean the same thing as if they said, "Since the Kingdom of Heaven has come near, repent.". . . [W]hen we refer the origin of repentance to faith we do not imagine some space of time during which it brings it to birth; but we mean to show that a man cannot apply himself seriously to repentance without knowing himself to belong to God. But no one is truly persuaded that he belongs to God unless he has first recognized God's grace.

3.3.3   *Mortification and vivification*

Certain men well versed in penance, even long before these times, meaning to speak simply and sincerely according to the rule of Scripture, said that it consists of two parts: mortification and vivification. Mortification they explain as sorrow of soul and dread conceived from the recognition of sin and the awareness of divine judgment. . . .

This is the first part of repentance, commonly called "contrition." "Vivification" they understand as the consolation that arises out of faith. That is, when a man is laid low by the consciousness of sin and stricken by the fear of God, and afterward looks to the goodness of God—to his mercy, grace, salvation, which is through Christ—he raises himself up, he takes heart, he recovers courage, and as it were, returns from death to life. . . . It means . . . the desire to live in a holy and devoted manner, a desire arising from rebirth; as if it were said that man dies to himself that he may begin to live to God.

(Repentance defined: explanation of its elements,   3.3.5–9
mortification of the flesh and vivification of the spirit)

Definition   3.3.5

I am aware of the fact that the whole of conversion to God is understood under the term "repentance," and faith is not the least part of conversion; but in what sense this is so will very readily appear when its force and nature are explained. The Hebrew word for "repentance" is derived from conversion or return; the Greek word, from change of mind or of intention. And the thing itself corresponds closely to the etymology of both words. The meaning is that, departing from ourselves, we turn to God, and having taken off our former mind, we put on a new. On this account, in my judgment, repentance can thus be well defined: it is the true turning of our life to God, a turning that arises from a pure and earnest fear of him; and it consists in the mortification of our flesh and of the old man, and in the vivification of the Spirit.

Mortification and vivification as component parts of repentance   3.3.8

It remains for us to explain our statement that repentance consists of two parts: namely, mortification of the flesh and vivification of the spirit.

Rebirth in Christ!   3.3.9

Both things happen to us by participation in Christ. For if we truly partake in his death, "our old man is crucified by his power, and the body of sin perishes" [Rom. 6:6 p.], that the corruption of original nature may no longer thrive. If we share in his resurrection, through it we are raised up into newness of life to correspond with the righteousness of God. Therefore, in a word, I interpret repentance as regeneration, whose sole end is to restore in us the image of God that

had been disfigured and all but obliterated through Adam's transgression. . . . I say, the closer any man comes to the likeness of God,
the more the image of God shines in him. In order that believers may
reach this goal, God assigns to them a race of repentance, which they
are to run throughout their lives.

3.3.10–15   *(Believers experience sanctification, but not sinless perfection in this life)*

3.3.10   *Believers are still sinners*

Thus, then, are the children of God freed through regeneration from
bondage to sin. Yet they do not obtain full possession of freedom so
as to feel no more annoyance from their flesh, but there still remains
in them a continuing occasion for struggle whereby they may be
exercised; and not only be exercised, but also better learn their own
weakness. . . .

We accordingly teach that in the saints, until they are divested of
mortal bodies, there is always sin; for in their flesh there resides that
depravity of inordinate desiring which contends against righteousness.

3.3.11   *In believers sin has lost its dominion; but it still dwells in them*

God is said to purge his church of all sin, in that through baptism he
promises that grace of deliverance, and fulfills it in his elect [Eph.
5:26–27]. This statement we refer to the guilt of sin, rather than to the
very substance of sin. God truly carries this out by regenerating his
own people, so that the sway of sin is abolished in them. For the Spirit
dispenses a power whereby they may gain the upper hand and
become victors in the struggle. But sin ceases only to reign; it does not
also cease to dwell in them. Accordingly, we say that the old man was
so crucified [Rom. 6:6], and the law of sin [cf. Rom. 8:2] so abolished
in the children of God, that some vestiges remain; not to rule over
them, but to humble them by the consciousness of their own weakness. And we, indeed, admit that these traces are not imputed, as if
they did not exist; but at the same time we contend that this comes to
pass through the mercy of God, so that the saints—otherwise
deservedly sinners and guilty before God—are freed from this guilt.

3.3.12   *What does "natural corruption" mean?*

All man's faculties are, on account of the depravity of nature, so vitiated and corrupted that in all his actions persistent disorder and
intemperance threaten because these inclinations cannot be separated
from such lack of restraint. Accordingly, we contend that they are

vicious. Or, if you would have the matter summed up in fewer words, we teach that all human desires are evil, and charge them with sin— not in that they are natural, but because they are inordinate. Moreover, we hold that they are inordinate because nothing pure or sincere can come forth from a corrupt and polluted nature.

Repentance according to II Cor. 7:11

3.3.15

It is for a very good reason that the apostle enumerates seven causes, effects, or parts in his description of repentance. They are earnestness or carefulness, excuse, indignation, fear, longing, zeal, and avenging [II Cor. 7:11].

(The fruits of repentance: holiness of life, confession and remission of sins; repentance is lifelong)

3.3.16–20

Outward and inward repentance

3.3.16

Now we can understand the nature of the fruits of repentance: the duties of piety toward God, of charity toward men, and in the whole of life, holiness and purity.

Repentance and forgiveness are interrelated

3.3.19

Now if it is true—a fact abundantly clear—that the whole of the gospel is contained under these two headings, repentance and forgiveness of sins, do we not see that the Lord freely justifies his own in order that he may at the same time restore them to true righteousness by sanctification of his Spirit? . . . Repentance is preached in the name of Christ when, through the teaching of the gospel, men hear that all their thoughts, all their inclinations, all their efforts, are corrupt and vicious. Accordingly, they must be reborn if they would enter the Kingdom of Heaven. Forgiveness of sins is preached when men are taught that for them Christ became redemption, righteousness, salvation, and life [I Cor. 1:30], by whose name they are freely accounted righteous and innocent in God's sight.

(Sins for which there is no repentance or pardon)

3.3.21–25

Unpardonable sin

3.3.22

I say, therefore, that they sin against the Holy Spirit who, with evil intention, resist God's truth, although by its brightness they are so touched that they cannot claim ignorance. Such resistance alone constitutes this sin.

3.6.1   *Plan of the treatise*

The object of regeneration, as we have said, is to manifest in the life of
believers a harmony and agreement between God's righteousness
and their obedience, and thus to confirm the adoption that they have
received as sons [Gal. 4:5; cf. II Peter 1:10].

The law of God contains in itself that newness by which his image
can be restored in us. But because our slowness needs many goads
and helps, it will be profitable to assemble from various passages of
Scripture a pattern for the conduct of life in order that those who
heartily repent may not err in their zeal.

Motives for the Christian life

Now this Scriptural instruction of which we speak has two main aspects. The first is that the love of righteousness, to which we are otherwise not at all inclined by nature, may be instilled and established in our hearts; the second, that a rule be set forth for us that does not let us wander about in our zeal for righteousness. . . . From what foundation may righteousness better arise than from the Scriptural warning that we must be made holy because our God is holy [Lev. 19:2; I Peter 1:15–16]?

The Christian life receives its strongest motive to God's work through the person and redemptive act of Christ

And to wake us more effectively, Scripture shows that God the Father, as he has reconciled us to himself in his Christ [cf. II Cor. 5:18], has in him stamped for us the likeness [cf. Heb. 1:3] to which he would have us conform. . . . Scripture draws its exhortation from the true fountain. It not only enjoins us to refer our life to God, its author, to whom it is bound; but after it has taught that we have degenerated from the true origin and condition of our creation, it also adds that Christ, through whom we return into favor with God, has been set before us as an example, whose pattern we ought to express in our life.

The Christian life is not a matter of the tongue but of the inmost heart

Imperfection and endeavor of the Christian life

I do not insist that the moral life of a Christian man breathe nothing but the very gospel, yet this ought to be desired, and we must strive toward it. But I do not so strictly demand evangelical perfection that I would not acknowledge as a Christian one who has not yet attained it. For thus all would be excluded from the church, since no one is found who is not far removed from it, while many have advanced a little toward it whom it would nevertheless be unjust to cast away. . . .

But no one in this earthly prison of the body has sufficient strength to press on with due eagerness, and weakness so weighs down the greater number that, with wavering and limping and even creeping along the ground, they move at a feeble rate. Let each one of us, then, proceed according to the measure of his puny capacity and set out upon the journey we have begun. No one shall set out so inauspiciously as not daily to make some headway, though it be slight. Therefore, let us not cease so to act that we may make some unceasing progress in the way of the Lord. And let us not despair at the slightness of our success; for even though attainment may not correspond to desire, when today outstrips yesterday the effort is not lost. Only let us look toward our mark with sincere simplicity and aspire to our goal; not fondly flattering ourselves, nor excusing our own evil deeds, but with continuous effort striving toward this end: that we may surpass ourselves in goodness until we attain to goodness itself. It is this, indeed, which through the whole course of life we seek and follow. But we shall attain it only when we have cast off the weakness of the body, and are received into full fellowship with him.

3.7   THE SUM OF THE CHRISTIAN LIFE: THE DENIAL OF OURSELVES

3.7.1–3   *(The Christian philosophy of unworldliness and self-denial;*
           we are not our own, we are God's)

3.7.1   *We are not our own masters, but belong to God*

Even though the law of the Lord provides the finest and best-disposed method of ordering a man's life, it seemed good to the Heavenly Teacher to shape his people by an even more explicit plan to that rule which he had set forth in the law. Here, then, is the beginning of this plan: the duty of believers is "to present their bodies to God as a living sacrifice, holy and acceptable to him," and in this consists the lawful worship of him [Rom. 12:1]. . . . [W]e are consecrated and dedicated to God in order that we may thereafter think, speak, meditate, and do, nothing except to his glory. . . .

We are not our own: let not our reason nor our will, therefore, sway our plans and deeds. We are not our own: let us therefore not set it as our goal to seek what is expedient for us according to the flesh. We are not our own: in so far as we can, let us therefore forget ourselves and all that is ours.

Conversely, we are God's: let us therefore live for him and die for him. We are God's: let his wisdom and will therefore rule all our actions. We are God's: let all the parts of our life accordingly strive toward him as our only lawful goal [Rom. 14:8; cf. I Cor. 6:19].

Let this therefore be the first step, that a man depart from himself in order that he may apply the whole force of his ability in the service of the Lord. I call "service" not only what lies in obedience to God's Word but what turns the mind of man, empty of its own carnal sense, wholly to the bidding of God's Spirit.

3.7.2   *Self-denial through devotion to God*

From this also follows this second point: that we seek not the things that are ours but those which are of the Lord's will and will serve to advance his glory. This is also evidence of great progress: that, almost forgetful of ourselves, surely subordinating our self-concern, we try faithfully to devote our zeal to God and his commandments.

(The principle of self-denial in our relations with our fellow men)   3.7.4–7

Self-denial gives us the right attitude toward our fellow men   3.7.4

Let us, then, unremittingly examining our faults, call ourselves back to humility. Thus nothing will remain in us to puff us up; but there will be much occasion to be cast down. On the other hand, we are bidden so to esteem and regard whatever gifts of God we see in other men that we may honor those men in whom they reside. For it would be great depravity on our part to deprive them of that honor which the Lord has bestowed upon them. But we are taught to overlook their faults, certainly not flatteringly to cherish them; but not on account of such faults to revile men whom we ought to cherish with good will and honor. Thus it will come about that, whatever man we deal with, we shall treat him not only moderately and modestly but also cordially and as a friend. You will never attain true gentleness except by one path: a heart imbued with lowliness and with reverence for others.

Self-renunciation leads to proper helpfulness toward our neighbors   3.7.5

Now, in seeking to benefit one's neighbor, how difficult it is to do one's duty! . . . Unless you give up all thought of self and, so to speak, get out of yourself, you will accomplish nothing here. . . . But Scripture, to lead us by the hand to this, warns that whatever benefits we obtain from the Lord have been entrusted to us on this condition: that they be applied to the common good of the church. And therefore the lawful use of all benefits consists in a liberal and kindly sharing of them with others. No surer rule and no more valid exhortation to keep it could be devised than when we are taught that all the gifts we possess have been bestowed by God and entrusted to us on condition that they be distributed for our neighbors' benefit [cf. I Pet. 4:10]. . . .

So, too, whatever a godly man can do he ought to be able to do for his brothers, providing for himself in no way other than to have his mind intent upon the common upbuilding of the church. Let this, therefore, be our rule for generosity and beneficence: We are the stewards of everything God has conferred on us by which we are able to help our neighbor, and are required to render account of our stewardship. Moreover, the only right stewardship is that which is tested by the rule of love. Thus it will come about that we shall not only join zeal for another's benefit with care for our own advantage, but shall subordinate the latter to the former. . . .

3.7.6   *Love of neighbor is not dependent upon manner of men but looks to God*

Scripture helps in the best way when it teaches that we are not to consider that men merit of themselves but to look upon the image of God
in all men, to which we owe all honor and love. However, it is among
members of the household of faith that this same image is more carefully to be noted [Gal. 6:10], in so far as it has been renewed and
restored through the Spirit of Christ. Therefore, whatever man you
meet who needs your aid, you have no reason to refuse to help him.
Say, "He is a stranger"; but the Lord has given him a mark that ought
to be familiar to you, by virtue of the fact that he forbids you to
despise your own flesh [Isa. 58:7, Vg.]. Say, "He is contemptible and
worthless"; but the Lord shows him to be one to whom he has
deigned to give the beauty of his image. . . . Now if he has not only
deserved no good at your hand, but has also provoked you by unjust
acts and curses, not even this is just reason why you should cease to
embrace him in love and to perform the duties of love on his behalf
[Matt. 6:14; 18:35; Luke 17:3]. . . . Assuredly there is but one way in
which to achieve what is not merely difficult but utterly against human
nature: to love those who hate us, to repay their evil deeds with benefits, to return blessings for reproaches [Matt. 5:44]. It is that we
remember not to consider men's evil intention but to look upon the
image of God in them, which cancels and effaces their transgressions,
and with its beauty and dignity allures us to love and embrace them.

3.7.7   *The outward work of love is not sufficient, but it is intention that counts!*

This mortification, then, will take place in us only if we fulfill the
duties of love. Now he who merely performs all the duties of love
does not fulfill them, even though he overlooks none; but he, rather,
fulfills them who does this from a sincere feeling of love. . . . [E]ach
man will so consider with himself that in all his greatness he is a
debtor to his neighbors, and that he ought in exercising kindness
toward them to set no other limit than the end of his resources; these,
as widely as they are extended, ought to have their limits set according to the rule of love.

3.7.8–10 *(The principle of self-denial in our relation to God)*

3.7.8   *Self-denial toward God: devotion to his will!*

Godly men must hold to this path. First of all, let them neither desire
nor hope for, nor contemplate, any other way of prospering than by
the Lord's blessing. Upon this, then, let them safely and confidently

throw themselves and rest. For however beautifully the flesh may seem to suffice unto itself, while it either strives by its own effort for honors and riches or relies upon its diligence, or is aided by the favor of men, yet it is certain that all these things are nothing; nor will we benefit at all, either by skill or by labor, except in so far as the Lord prospers them both.

Trust in God's blessing only   3.7.9

Suppose we believe that every means toward a prosperous and desirable outcome rests upon the blessing of God alone; and that, when this is absent, all sorts of misery and calamity dog us. It remains for us not greedily to strive after riches and honors—whether relying upon our own dexterity of wit or our own diligence, or depending upon the favor of men, or having confidence in vainly imagined fortune—but for us always to look to the Lord so that by his guidance we may be led to whatever lot he has provided for us. Thus it will first come to pass that we shall not dash out to seize upon riches and usurp honors through wickedness and by stratagems and evil arts, or greed, to the injury of our neighbors; but pursue only those enterprises which do not lead us away from innocence.

Self-denial helps us bear adversity   3.7.10

And for godly minds the peace and forbearance we have spoken of ought not to rest solely in this point; but it must also be extended to every occurrence to which the present life is subject. Therefore, he alone has duly denied himself who has so totally resigned himself to the Lord that he permits every part of his life to be governed by God's will. He who will be thus composed in mind, whatever happens, will not consider himself miserable nor complain of his lot with ill will toward God. . . . [T]he rule of piety is that God's hand alone is the judge and governor of fortune, good or bad, and that it does not rush about with heedless force, but with most orderly justice deals out good as well as ill to us.

BEARING THE CROSS, A PART OF SELF-DENIAL   3.8

(We are to take up our cross, as followers of Christ)   3.8.1–2

Christ's cross and ours   3.8.1

But it behooves the godly mind to climb still higher, to the height to which Christ calls his disciples: that each must bear his own cross

[Matt.16:24]. For whomever the Lord has adopted and deemed worthy of his fellowship ought to prepare themselves for a hard, toilsome, and unquiet life, crammed with very many and various kinds of evil. It is the Heavenly Father's will thus to exercise them so as to put his own children to a definite test. Beginning with Christ, his first-born, he follows this plan with all his children. For even though that Son was beloved above the rest, and in him the Father's mind was well pleased [Matt. 3:17 and 17:5], yet we see that far from being treated indulgently or softly, to speak the truth, while he dwelt on earth he was not only tried by a perpetual cross but his whole life was nothing but a sort of perpetual cross. The apostle notes the reason: that it behooved him to "learn obedience through what he suffered" [Heb. 5:8]. . . .

Hence also in harsh and difficult conditions, regarded as adverse and evil, a great comfort comes to us: we share Christ's sufferings in order that as he has passed from a labyrinth of all evils into heavenly glory, we may in like manner be led through various tribulations to the same glory [Acts 14:22].

3.8.2   *The cross leads us to perfect trust in God's power*

Besides this, our Lord had no need to undertake the bearing of the cross except to attest and prove his obedience to the Father. But as for us, there are many reasons why we must pass our lives under a continual cross. . . . [W]e readily esteem our virtue above its due measure. And we do not doubt, whatever happens, that against all difficulties it will remain unbroken and unconquered. Hence we are lifted up into stupid and empty confidence in the flesh; and relying on it, we are then insolently proud against God himself, as if our own powers were sufficient without his grace.

He can best restrain this arrogance when he proves to us by experience not only the great incapacity but also the frailty under which we labor. Therefore, he afflicts us either with disgrace or poverty, or bereavement, or disease, or other calamities. Utterly unequal to bearing these, in so far as they touch us, we soon succumb to them. Thus humbled, we learn to call upon his power, which alone makes us stand fast under the weight of afflictions. But even the most holy persons, however much they may recognize that they stand not through their own strength but through God's grace, are too sure of their own fortitude and constancy unless by the testing of the cross he bring them into a deeper knowledge of himself.

3.8.3–6   *(This is needful to teach us patience and obedience)*

The cross permits us to experience God's faithfulness   3.8.3
and gives us hope for the future

And this is what Paul teaches: "Tribulations produce patience; and patience, tried character" [Rom. 5:3–4, cf. Vg.]. That God has promised to be with believers in tribulation [cf. II Cor. 1:4] they experience to be true, while, supported by his hand, they patiently endure—an endurance quite unattainable by their own effort. The saints, therefore, through forbearance experience the fact that God, when there is need, provides the assistance that he has promised.

The cross trains us to patience and obedience   3.8.4

The Lord also has another purpose for afflicting his people: to test their patience and to instruct them to obedience. Not that they can manifest any other obedience to him save what he has given them. But it so pleases him by unmistakable proofs to make manifest and clear the graces which he has conferred upon the saints, that these may not lie idle, hidden within.

The cross as medicine   3.8.5

Some are tried by one kind of cross, others by another. But since the heavenly physician treats some more gently but cleanses others by harsher remedies, while he wills to provide for the health of all, he yet leaves no one free and untouched, because he knows that all, to a man, are diseased.

The cross as fatherly chastisement   3.8.6

Besides this, it is needful that our most merciful Father should not only anticipate our weakness but also often correct past transgressions so that he may keep us in lawful obedience to himself. Accordingly, whenever we are afflicted, remembrance of our past life ought immediately to come to mind; so we shall doubtless find that we have committed something deserving this sort of chastisement. . . . When we recognize the Father's rod, is it not our duty to show ourselves obedient and teachable children rather than, in arrogance, to imitate desperate men who have become hardened in their evil deeds? When we have fallen away from him, God destroys us unless by reproof he recalls us. Thus he rightly says that if we are without discipline we are illegitimate children, not sons [Heb. 12:8]. We are, then, most perverse if when he declares his benevolence to us and the care that he takes for our salvation, we cannot bear him. Scripture teaches that this is the difference between unbelievers and believers: the former, like slaves of inveterate and double-dyed wickedness, with chastisement become only worse and more obstinate. But the latter, like freeborn sons, attain repentance. Now you must choose in which group you would prefer to be numbered.

3.8.7–8   *(Bearing the cross in persecution and other calamities)*

3.8.7   *Suffering for righteousness' sake*

Now, to suffer persecution for righteousness' sake is a singular comfort. For it ought to occur to us how much honor God bestows upon us in thus furnishing us with the special badge of his soldiery. I say that not only they who labor for the defense of the gospel but they who in any way maintain the cause of righteousness suffer persecution for righteousness. . . . If, being innocent and of good conscience, we are stripped of our possessions by the wickedness of impious folk, we are indeed reduced to penury among men. But in God's presence in heaven our true riches are thus increased. If we are cast out of our own house, then we will be the more intimately received into God's family. If we are vexed and despised, we but take all the firmer root in Christ. If we are branded with disgrace and ignominy, we but have a fuller place in the Kingdom of God. If we are slain, entrance into the blessed life will thus be open to us. Let us be ashamed to esteem less than the shadowy and fleeting allurements of the present life, those things on which the Lord has set so great a value.

3.8.9–11   *(The Christian meets suffering as sent by God,*
but with no Stoic insensibility)

3.9   MEDITATION ON THE FUTURE LIFE

3.9.1–2   *(By our tribulations God weans us*
from excessive love of this present life)

3.9.1   *The vanity of this life*

Whatever kind of tribulation presses upon us, we must ever look to this end: to accustom ourselves to contempt for the present life and to be aroused thereby to meditate upon the future life. For since God knows best how much we are inclined by nature to a brutish love of this world, he uses the fittest means to draw us back and to shake off our sluggishness, lest we cleave too tenaciously to that love. . . .

Then only do we rightly advance by the discipline of the cross, when we learn that this life, judged in itself, is troubled, turbulent, unhappy in countless ways, and in no respect clearly happy; that all those things which are judged to be its goods are uncertain, fleeting, vain, and vitiated by many intermingled evils. From this, at the same time, we conclude that in this life we are to seek and hope for nothing but struggle; when we think of our crown, we are to raise our eyes to heaven. For this we must believe: that the mind is never seriously aroused to desire and ponder the life to come unless it be previously imbued with contempt for the present life.

(A right estimate of the present life, which is transient   3.9.3–6
and unsatisfying, leads us to meditate on the life to come)

Gratitude for earthly life!   3.9.3

But let believers accustom themselves to a contempt of the present life that engenders no hatred of it or ingratitude against God. Indeed, this life, however crammed with infinite miseries it may be, is still rightly to be counted among those blessings of God which are not to be spurned. . . .

We begin in the present life, through various benefits, to taste the sweetness of the divine generosity in order to whet our hope and desire to seek after the full revelation of this. When we are certain that the earthly life we live is a gift of God's kindness, as we are beholden to him for it we ought to remember it and be thankful. Then we shall come in good time to consider its most unhappy condition in order that we may, indeed, be freed from too much desire of it, to which, as has been said, we are of ourselves inclined by nature.

The right longing for eternal life   3.9.4

Let the aim of believers in judging mortal life, then, be that while they understand it to be of itself nothing but misery, they may with greater eagerness and dispatch betake themselves wholly to meditate upon that eternal life to come. When it comes to a comparison with the life to come, the present life can not only be safely neglected but, compared to the former, must be utterly despised and loathed. For, if heaven is our homeland, what else is the earth but our place of exile? . . . Therefore, if the earthly life be compared with the heavenly, it is doubtless to be at once despised and trampled under foot. Of course it is never to be hated except in so far as it holds us subject to sin; although not even hatred of that condition may ever properly be turned against life itself. In any case, it is still fitting for us to be so affected either by weariness or hatred of it that, desiring its end, we may also be prepared to abide in it at the Lord's pleasure, so that our weariness may be far from all murmuring and impatience. For it is like a sentry post at which the Lord has posted us, which we must hold until he recalls us. . . . Therefore, if it befits us to live and die to the Lord, let us leave to his decision the hour of our death and life, but in such a way that we may both burn with the zeal for death and be constant in meditation. But in comparison with the immortality to come, let us despise this life and long to renounce it, on account of bondage of sin, whenever it shall please the Lord.

3.9.5   *Against the fear of death!*

But monstrous it is that many who boast themselves Christians are gripped by such a great fear of death, rather than a desire for it, that they tremble at the least mention of it, as of something utterly dire and disastrous. . . .

Let us, however, consider this settled: that no one has made progress in the school of Christ who does not joyfully await the day of death and final resurrection. . . . [E]ven though the blind and stupid desire of the flesh resists, let us not hesitate to await the Lord's coming, not only with longing, but also with groaning and sighs, as the happiest thing of all. He will come to us as Redeemer, and rescuing us from this boundless abyss of all evils and miseries, he will lead us into that blessed inheritance of his life and glory.

3.9.6   *The comfort prepared for believers by aspiration for the life to come*

If believers' eyes are turned to the power of the resurrection, in their hearts the cross of Christ will at last triumph over the devil, flesh, sin, and wicked men.

3.10   HOW WE MUST USE THE PRESENT LIFE AND ITS HELPS

3.10.1–2   *(The good things of this life are to be enjoyed as gifts of God)*

3.10.1   *Double danger: mistaken strictness and mistaken laxity*

Scripture at the same time duly informs us what is the right use of earthly benefits—a matter not to be neglected in the ordering of our life. For if we are to live, we have also to use those helps necessary for living. And we also cannot avoid those things which seem to serve delight more than necessity. Therefore we must hold to a measure so as to use them with a clear conscience, whether for necessity or for delight. . . . If we must simply pass through this world, there is no doubt we ought to use its good things in so far as they help rather than hinder our course.

The main principle   3.10.2

Let this be our principle: that the use of God's gifts is not wrongly directed when it is referred to that end to which the Author himself created and destined them for us, since he created them for our good, not for our ruin. . . . Has the Lord clothed the flowers with the great beauty that greets our eyes, the sweetness of smell that is wafted upon our nostrils, and yet will it be unlawful for our eyes to be affected by that beauty, or our sense of smell by the sweetness of that odor? What? Did he not so distinguish colors as to make some more lovely than others? What? Did he not endow gold and silver, ivory and marble, with a loveliness that renders them more precious than other metals or stones? Did he not, in short, render many things attractive to us, apart from their necessary use?

(We are not to use these blessings indulgently,   3.10.3–6
or to seek wealth greedily, but to serve dutifully in our calling)

A look at the Giver of the gift   3.10.3
prevents narrow-mindedness and immoderation

Away, then, with that inhuman philosophy which, while conceding only a necessary use of creatures, not only malignantly deprives us of the lawful fruit of God's beneficence but cannot be practiced unless it robs a man of all his senses and degrades him to a block.

Aspiration to eternal life   3.10.4
also determines aright our outward conduct of life

But there is no surer or more direct course than that which we receive from contempt of the present life and meditation upon heavenly immortality. For from this two rules follow: those who use this world should be so affected as if they did not use it. . . . The other rule is that they should know how to bear poverty peaceably and patiently, as well as to bear abundance moderately.

Therefore, even though the freedom of believers in external matters is not to be restricted to a fixed formula, yet it is surely subject to this law: to indulge oneself as little as possible; but, on the contrary, with unflagging effort of mind to insist upon cutting off all show of superfluous wealth, not to mention licentiousness, and diligently to guard against turning helps into hindrances.

3.10.5 *Frugality, earthly possessions held in trust*

The second rule will be: they who have narrow and slender resources should know how to go without things patiently, lest they be troubled by an immoderate desire for them. If they keep this rule of moderation, they will make considerable progress in the Lord's school. . . .

Scripture has a third rule with which to regulate the use of earthly things. Of it we said something when we discussed the precepts of love. It decrees that all those things were so given to us by the kindness of God, and so destined for our benefit, that they are, as it were, entrusted to us, and we must one day render account of them. Thus, therefore, we must so arrange it that this saying may continually resound in our ears: "Render account of your stewardship" [Luke 16:2].

3.10.6 *The Lord's calling a basis of our way of life*

Finally, this point is to be noted: the Lord bids each one of us in all life's actions to look to his calling. For he knows with what great restlessness human nature flames, with what fickleness it is borne hither and thither, how its ambition longs to embrace various things at once. Therefore, lest through our stupidity and rashness everything be turned topsy-turvy, he has appointed duties for every man in his particular way of life. And that no one may thoughtlessly transgress his limits, he has named these various kinds of living "callings." Therefore each individual has his own kind of living assigned to him by the Lord as a sort of sentry post so that he may not heedlessly wander about throughout life. . . .

From this will arise also a singular consolation: that no task will be so sordid and base, provided you obey your calling in it, that it will not shine and be reckoned very precious in God's sight.

3.11 JUSTIFICATION BY FAITH: FIRST THE DEFINITION OF THE WORD AND OF THE MATTER

3.11.1–4 *(Justification and regeneration, the terms defined)*

3.11.1 *Place and meaning of the doctrine of "justification"*

Christ was given to us by God's generosity, to be grasped and possessed by us in faith. By partaking of him, we principally receive a double grace: namely, that being reconciled to God through Christ's blamelessness, we may have in heaven instead of a Judge a gracious Father; and secondly, that sanctified by Christ's spirit we may cultivate blamelessness and purity of life. Of regeneration, indeed, the second of these gifts, I have said what seemed sufficient. The theme of justification was therefore more lightly touched upon because it was more to the point to understand first how little devoid of good works is the faith, through which alone we obtain free righteousness by the mercy of God; and what is the nature of the good works of the saints, with which part of this question is concerned. Therefore we must now discuss these matters thoroughly. And we must so discuss them as to bear in mind that this is the main hinge on which religion turns.

The concept of justification   3.11.2

He is said to be justified in God's sight who is both reckoned righteous in God's judgment and has been accepted on account of his righteousness. Indeed, as iniquity is abominable to God, so no sinner can find favor in his eyes in so far as he is a sinner and so long as he is reckoned as such. Accordingly, wherever there is sin, there also the wrath and vengeance of God show themselves. Now he is justified who is reckoned in the condition not of a sinner, but of a righteous man; and for that reason, he stands firm before God's judgment seat while all sinners fall. . . . On the contrary, justified by faith is he who, excluded from the righteousness of works, grasps the righteousness of Christ through faith, and clothed in it, appears in God's sight not as a sinner but as a righteous man.

Therefore, we explain justification simply as the acceptance with which God receives us into his favor as righteous men. And we say that it consists in the remission of sins and the imputation of Christ's righteousness.

Justification as gracious acceptance by God and as forgiveness of sins   3.11.4

The best passage of all on this matter is the one in which he teaches that the sum of the gospel embassy is to reconcile us to God, since God is willing to receive us into grace through Christ, not counting our sins against us [II Cor. 5:18–20]. Let my readers carefully ponder the whole passage. For a little later Paul adds by way of explanation: "Christ, who was without sin, was made sin for us" [II Cor. 5:21], to designate the means of reconciliation [cf. vs. 18–19]. Doubtless, he means by the word "reconciled" nothing but "justified." And surely, what he teaches elsewhere—that "we are made righteous by Christ's obedience" [Rom. 5:19 p.]—could not stand unless we are reckoned righteous before God in Christ and apart from ourselves.

3.11.5–12   *(Refutation of Osiander's doctrine of "essential righteousness")*

3.11.9   *Justification as the work of the Mediator*

Christ is, as it were, a fountain, open to us, from which we may draw what otherwise would lie unprofitably hidden in that deep and secret spring, which comes forth to us in the person of the Mediator. In this way and sense, I do not deny that Christ, as he is God and man, justifies us; and also that this work is the common task of the Father and the Holy Spirit; finally, that righteousness of which Christ makes us partakers with himself is the eternal righteousness of the eternal God.

3.11.10   *What is the nature of our union with Christ?*

I confess that we are deprived of this utterly incomparable good until Christ is made ours. Therefore, that joining together of Head and members, that indwelling of Christ in our hearts—in short, that mystical union—are accorded by us the highest degree of importance, so that Christ, having been made ours, makes us sharers with him in the gifts with which he has been endowed. We do not, therefore, contemplate him outside ourselves from afar in order that his righteousness may be imputed to us but because we put on Christ and are engrafted into his body—in short, because he deigns to make us one with him. For this reason, we glory that we have fellowship of righteousness with him.

3.11.13–20   *(Refutation of Scholastic doctrines of good works as effective for justification)*

3.11.13   *Righteousness by faith and righteousness by works*

But a great part of mankind imagine that righteousness is composed of faith and works. Let us also, to begin with, show that faith righteousness so differs from works righteousness that when one is established the other has to be overthrown. . . . If by establishing our own righteousness we shake off the righteousness of God, to attain the latter we must indeed completely do away with the former. He also shows this very thing when he states that our boasting is not excluded by law but by faith [Rom. 3:27]. . . . From this it follows that so long as any particle of works righteousness remains some occasion for boasting remains with us. Now, if faith excludes all boasting, works righteousness can in no way be associated with faith righteousness. . . . But righteousness according to grace is owed to faith. Therefore it does not arise from the merits of works. Farewell, then, to the dream of those who think up a righteousness flowing together out of faith and works.

Likewise, the works of the regenerated can procure no justification   3.11.14

The Sophists, who make game and sport in their corrupting of Scripture and their empty caviling, think they have a subtle evasion. For they explain "works" as meaning those which men not yet reborn do only according to the letter by the effort of their own free will, apart from Christ's grace. But they deny that these refer to spiritual works. For, according to them, man is justified by both faith and works provided they are not his own works but the gifts of Christ and the fruit of regeneration. . . .

Moreover, we shall see afterward, in its proper place, that the benefits of Christ—sanctification and righteousness—are different. From this it follows that not even spiritual works come into account when the power of justifying is ascribed to faith.

Our justification according to the judgment of Scripture   3.11.16

Scripture, when it speaks of faith righteousness, leads us to something far different: namely, to turn aside from the contemplation of our own works and look solely upon God's mercy and Christ's perfection. Indeed, it presents this order of justification: to begin with, God deigns to embrace the sinner with his pure and freely given goodness, finding nothing in him except his miserable condition to prompt Him to mercy, since he sees man utterly void and bare of good works; and so he seeks in himself the reason to benefit man. Then God touches the sinner with a sense of his goodness in order that he, despairing of his own works, may ground the whole of his salvation in God's mercy. This is the experience of faith through which the sinner comes into possession of his salvation when from the teaching of the gospel he acknowledges that he has been reconciled to God: that with Christ's righteousness interceding and forgiveness of sins accomplished he is justified. And although regenerated by the Spirit of God, he ponders the everlasting righteousness laid up for him not in the good works to which he inclines but in the sole righteousness of Christ.

Faith righteousness and law righteousness according to Paul   3.11.17

Here we should recall to mind the relation that we have previously established between faith and the gospel. For faith is said to justify because it receives and embraces the righteousness offered in the gospel. Moreover, because righteousness is said to be offered through the gospel, all consideration of works is excluded.

3.11.18 *Justification not the wages of works, but a free gift*

It is clear that those who are justified by faith are justified apart from the merit of works—in fact, without the merit of works. For faith receives that righteousness which the gospel bestows. Now the gospel differs from the law in that it does not link righteousness to works but lodges it solely in God's mercy.

3.11.20 *"Works of the law"*

Also, they pointlessly strive after the foolish subtlety that we are justified by faith alone, which acts through love, so that righteousness depends upon love. Indeed, we confess with Paul that no other faith justifies "but faith working through love" [Gal. 5:6]. But it does not take its power to justify from that working of love. Indeed, it justifies in no other way but in that it leads us into fellowship with the righteousness of Christ.

3.11.21–23 *(Sins are remitted only through the righteousness of Christ)*

3.11.21 *Justification, reconciliation, forgiveness of sins*

Now let us examine how true that statement is which is spoken in the definition, that the righteousness of faith is reconciliation with God, which consists solely in the forgiveness of sins. We must always return to this axiom: the wrath of God rests upon all so long as they continue to be sinners. Isaiah has very well expressed it in these words: "The Lord's hand is not shortened, that it cannot save, or his ear dull, that it cannot hear; but your iniquities have made a separation between you and your God, and your sins have hid his face from you lest he hear" [Isa. 59:1–2]. We are told that sin is division between man and God, the turning of God's face away from the sinner; and it cannot happen otherwise, seeing that it is foreign to his righteousness to have any dealings with sin. For this reason, the apostle teaches that man is God's enemy until he is restored to grace through Christ [Rom. 5:8–10]. Thus, him whom he receives into union with himself the Lord is said to justify, because he cannot receive him into grace nor join him to himself unless he turns him from a sinner into a righteous man. We add that this is done through forgiveness of sins; for if those whom the Lord has reconciled to himself be judged by works, they will indeed still be found sinners, though they ought, nevertheless, to be freed and cleansed from sin. It is obvious, therefore, that those whom God embraces are made righteous solely by the fact that they are purified when their spots are washed away by forgiveness of sins. Consequently, such righteousness can be called, in a word, "remission of sins."

Righteous—not in ourselves but in Christ   3.11.23

It is also evident that we are justified before God solely by the intercession of Christ's righteousness. This is equivalent to saying that man is not righteous in himself but because the righteousness of Christ is communicated to him by imputation—something worth carefully noting. Indeed, that frivolous notion disappears, that man is justified by faith because by Christ's righteousness he shares the Spirit of God, by whom he is rendered righteous. This is too contrary to the above doctrine ever to be reconciled to it. And there is no doubt that he who is taught to seek righteousness outside himself is destitute of righteousness in himself. Moreover, the apostle most clearly asserts this when he writes: "He who knew not sin was made the atoning sacrifice of sin for us so that we might be made the righteousness of God in him" [II Cor. 5:21 p.].

You see that our righteousness is not in us but in Christ, that we possess it only because we are partakers in Christ; indeed, with him we possess all its riches. . . . For in such a way does the Lord Christ share his righteousness with us that, in some wonderful manner, he pours into us enough of his power to meet the judgment of God. . . . To declare that by him alone we are accounted righteous, what else is this but to lodge our righteousness in Christ's obedience, because the obedience of Christ is reckoned to us as if it were our own?

WE MUST LIFT UP OUR MINDS TO GOD'S JUDGMENT SEAT   3.12
THAT WE MAY BE FIRMLY CONVINCED OF HIS FREE JUSTIFICATION

(Justification in the light of the majesty and perfection of God)   3.12.1–3

(Conscience and self-criticism before God deprive us   3.12.4–8
of all claim to good works and lead us to embrace God's mercy)

TWO THINGS TO BE NOTED IN FREE JUSTIFICATION   3.13

Justification serves God's honor; and revelation, his justice   3.13.1

Here, indeed, we are especially to note two things: namely, that the Lord's glory should stand undiminished and, so to speak, in good repair, and that our consciences in the presence of his judgment should have peaceful rest and serene tranquillity.

3.13.2   *He who glories in his own righteousness robs God of his honor*

Thus the matter stands: we never truly glory in him unless we have utterly put off our own glory. On the other hand, we must hold this as a universal principle: whoever glories in himself, glories against God. . . .

To sum up, man cannot without sacrilege claim for himself even a crumb of righteousness, for just so much is plucked and taken away from the glory of God's righteousness.

3.13.3   *A glance at one's own righteousness provides no peace for the conscience*

Now if we ask in what way the conscience can be made quiet before God, we shall find the only way to be that unmerited righteousness be conferred upon us as a gift of God.

3.13.4   *Attention to one's own righteousness also nullifies the promises*

Scripture shows that God's promises are not established unless they are grasped with the full assurance of conscience. Wherever there is doubt or uncertainty, it pronounces them void. Again, it declares that these promises do nothing but vacillate and waver if they rest upon our own works. Therefore, righteousness must either depart from us or works must not be brought into account, but faith alone must have place, whose nature it is to prick up the ears and close the eyes—that is, to be intent upon the promise alone and to turn thought away from all worth or merit of man.

3.13.5   *Faith in God's free grace alone gives us*
peace of conscience and gladness in prayer

Believers should be convinced that their only ground of hope for the inheritance of a Heavenly Kingdom lies in the fact that, being engrafted in the body of Christ, they are freely accounted righteous. For, as regards justification, faith is something merely passive, bringing nothing of ours to the recovering of God's favor but receiving from Christ that which we lack.

3.14   THE BEGINNING OF JUSTIFICATION AND ITS CONTINUAL PROGRESS

3.14.1–6 *(Man in his natural state dead in sins and in need of redemption)*

Four classes of men with regard to justification

Let us examine what kind of righteousness is possible to man through the whole course of his life; let us, indeed, make a fourfold classification of it. For men are either (1) endowed with no knowledge of God and immersed in idolatry; or (2) initiated into the sacraments, yet by impurity of life denying God in their actions while they confess him with their lips, they belong to Christ only in name; or (3) they are hypocrites who conceal with empty pretenses their wickedness of heart; or (4) regenerated by God's Spirit, they make true holiness their concern. In the first instance, when they are to be judged according to their natural gifts, not one spark of good will be found in them from the top of their heads to the soles of their feet.

The virtues of unbelievers are God-given

I do not deny that all the notable endowments that manifest themselves among unbelievers are gifts of God. . . . All these virtues . . . are gifts of God, since nothing is in any way praiseworthy that does not come from him.

No true virtue without true faith

Yet what Augustine writes is nonetheless true: that all who are estranged from the religion of the one God, however admirable they may be regarded on account of their reputation for virtue, not only deserve no reward but rather punishment, because by the pollution of their hearts they defile God's good works. For even though they are God's instruments for the preservation of human society in righteousness, continence, friendship, temperance, fortitude, and prudence, yet they carry out these good works of God very badly. For they are restrained from evil-doing not by genuine zeal for good but either by mere ambition or by self-love, or some other perverse motive. Therefore, since by the very impurity of men's hearts these good works have been corrupted as from their source, they ought no more to be reckoned among virtues than the vices that commonly deceive on account of their affinity and likeness to virtue.

Without Christ there is no true holiness

Whatever a man thinks, plans, or carries out before he is reconciled to God through faith is accursed, not only of no value for righteousness, but surely deserving condemnation. Yet why do we argue over this as if it were something doubtful, when it has already been proved by the apostle's testimony that "without faith it is impossible for anyone to please God" [Heb. 11:6]?

3.14.7–8 *(Hypocrites and nominal Christians, under condemnation)*

3.14.8 *Person and work*

They have spoken very truly who have taught that favor with God is not obtained by anyone through works, but on the contrary works please him only when the person has previously found favor in his sight. . . . Therefore, purification of heart must precede, in order that those works which come forth from us may be favorably received by God. For the statement of Jeremiah is always in force, that the eyes of God have regard for truth [Jer. 5:3]. That it is faith alone, moreover, by which men's hearts are purified, the Holy Spirit has declared through the mouth of Peter [Acts 15:9]. From this it is evident that the first foundation lies in true and living faith.

3.14.9–11 *(Those who are regenerated, justified by faith alone)*

3.14.9 *Also, true believers do no good works of themselves*

Let us examine what righteousness is possessed by those whom we have placed in the fourth class. We confess that while through the intercession of Christ's righteousness God reconciles us to himself, and by free remission of sins accounts us righteous, his beneficence is at the same time joined with such a mercy that through his Holy Spirit he dwells in us and by his power the lusts of our flesh are each day more and more mortified; we are indeed sanctified, that is, consecrated to the Lord in true purity of life, with our hearts formed to obedience to the law. The end is that our especial will may be to serve his will and by every means to advance his glory alone.

But even while by the leading of the Holy Spirit we walk in the ways of the Lord, to keep us from forgetting ourselves and becoming puffed up, traces of our imperfection remain to give us occasion for humility. Scripture says: There is no righteous man, no man who will do good and not sin [Eccl. 7:21, Vg.; cf. I Kings 8:46]. What sort of righteousness will they obtain, then, from their works? First, I say that the best work that can be brought forward from them is still always spotted and corrupted with some impurity of the flesh, and has, so to speak, some dregs mixed with it.

3.14.11 *Believers' righteousness is always faith righteousness*

We must strongly insist upon these two points: first, that there never existed any work of a godly man which, if examined by God's stern judgment, would not deserve condemnation; secondly, if such a work were found (something not possible for man), it would still lose favor—weakened and stained as it is by the sins with which its author himself is surely burdened.

(Scholastic objections to justification by faith, and doctrine of the   3.14.12–21
supererogatory merits of the saints examined and refuted)

One who speaks of "supererogatory" works misunderstands   3.14.13
the sharpness of God's demand and the gravity of sin

If these things are true, surely no works of ours can of themselves render us acceptable and pleasing to God; nor can even the works themselves please him, except to the extent that a man, covered by the righteousness of Christ, pleases God and obtains forgiveness of his sins. For God has not promised the reward of life for particular works but he only declares that the man who does them shall live [Lev. 18:5].

No trust in works and no glory in works!   3.14.16

There are two plagues that we must especially banish from our minds: we must not put any confidence in the righteousness of works, and we must not ascribe to works any glory.

Works are God's gift and cannot   3.14.20
become the foundation of self-confidence for believers

We now see that the saints have not a confidence in works that either attributes anything to their merit, since they regard them solely as gifts of God from which they may recognize his goodness and as signs of the calling by which they realize their election, or in any degree diminishes the free righteousness that we attain in Christ, since it depends upon this and does not subsist without it.

BOASTING ABOUT THE MERITS OF WORKS DESTROYS OUR PRAISE   3.15
OF GOD FOR HAVING BESTOWED RIGHTEOUSNESS,
AS WELL AS OUR ASSURANCE OF SALVATION

(Doctrine of human merit in justification opposed by Augustine and   3.15.1–4
Bernard as well as by Scripture)

The whole value of good works comes from God's grace   3.15.3

Those good works which he has bestowed upon us the Lord calls "ours," and testifies they not only are acceptable to him but also will have their reward. It is our duty in return to be aroused by so great a promise, to take courage not to weary in well-doing [cf. Gal. 6:9; II Thess. 3:13], and to receive God's great kindness with true gratefulness. There is no doubt that whatever is praiseworthy in works is God's grace; there is not a drop that we ought by rights to ascribe to ourselves. If we truly and earnestly recognize this, not only will all confidence in merit vanish, but the very notion. We are not dividing the credit for good works between God and man, as the Sophists do, but we are preserving it whole, complete, and unimpaired for the Lord. . . . Good works, then, are pleasing to God and are not unfruitful for their doers. But they receive by way of reward the most ample benefits of God, not because they so deserve but because God's kindness has of itself set this value on them.

3.15.5–8   *(Rejection of the substitution of man's merit for Christ's)*

3.16   REFUTATION OF THE FALSE ACCUSATIONS BY WHICH
            THE PAPISTS TRY TO CAST ODIUM UPON THIS DOCTRINE

3.16.1   *Does the doctrine of justification do away with good works?*

For we dream neither of a faith devoid of good works nor of a justification that stands without them. This alone is of importance: having admitted that faith and good works must cleave together, we still lodge justification in faith, not in works. We have a ready explanation for doing this, provided we turn to Christ to whom our faith is directed and from whom it receives its full strength.

Why, then, are we justified by faith? Because by faith we grasp Christ's righteousness, by which alone we are reconciled to God. Yet you could not grasp this without at the same time grasping sanctification also. For he "is given unto us for righteousness, wisdom, sanctification, and redemption" [I Cor. 1:30]. Therefore Christ justifies no one whom he does not at the same time sanctify. These benefits are joined together by an everlasting and indissoluble bond, so that those whom he illumines by his wisdom, he redeems; those whom he redeems, he justifies; those whom he justifies, he sanctifies.

Since, therefore, it is solely by expending himself that the Lord gives us these benefits to enjoy, he bestows both of them at the same time, the one never without the other. Thus it is clear how true it is that we are justified not without works yet not through works, since in our sharing in Christ, which justifies us, sanctification is just as much included as righteousness.

Does the doctrine of justification stifle zeal for good works?   3.16.2

God's honor and God's mercy as motives for action: 3.16.3
subordination of works

The doctrine of justification as incitement to the sinful   3.16.4

THE AGREEMENT OF THE PROMISES OF THE LAW AND OF THE GOSPEL   3.17

(Works as related to the law: the instance of Cornelius)   3.17.1–5

In what sense the Lord is pleased with the good works of the regenerate   3.17.5

God's children are pleasing and lovable to him, since he sees in them the marks and features of his own countenance. For we have elsewhere taught that regeneration is a renewal of the divine image in us. Since, therefore, wherever God contemplates his own face, he both rightly loves it and holds it in honor, it is said with good reason that the lives of believers, framed to holiness and righteousness, are pleasing to him.

(Passages that relate justification to works examined)   3.17.6–15

Works acceptable only when sins have been pardoned   3.17.10

Therefore, as we ourselves, when we have been engrafted in Christ, are righteous in God's sight because our iniquities are covered by Christ's sinlessness, so our works are righteous and are thus regarded because whatever fault is otherwise in them is buried in Christ's purity, and is not charged to our account. Accordingly, we can deservedly say that by faith alone not only we ourselves but our works as well are justified.

The word "justify" used by James in a sense different from Paul's   3.17.12

We have not yet reached the end unless we discuss the other fallacy as well: namely, that James puts part of justification in works. If you would make James agree with the rest of Scripture and with himself, you must understand the word "justify" in another sense than Paul takes it. . . . It is as if he [James 2:21, 23—ed.] said: "Those who by true faith are righteous prove their righteousness by obedience and good works, not by a bare and imaginary mask of faith." To sum up, he is not discussing in what manner we are justified but demanding of believers a righteousness fruitful in good works. And as Paul contends that we are justified apart from the help of works, so James does not allow those who lack good works to be reckoned righteous.

3.18   WORKS RIGHTEOUSNESS IS WRONGLY INFERRED FROM REWARD

3.18.1–4   *(Passages referring to reward do not make works the cause of salvation)*

3.18.5–10   *(Answers to objections against this view)*

3.19   CHRISTIAN FREEDOM

3.19.1–3   *(Necessity of a doctrine of Christian freedom,*
             which has three parts, the first seen in Gal[atians])

3.19.2   *Freedom from the law*

Christian freedom, in my opinion, consists of three parts. The first: that the consciences of believers, in seeking assurance of their justification before God, should rise above and advance beyond the law, forgetting all law righteousness.... The whole life of Christians ought to be a sort of practice of godliness, for we have been called to sanctification [I Thess. 4:7; cf. Eph. 1:4; I Thess. 4:3]. Here it is the function of the law, by warning men of their duty, to arouse them to a zeal for holiness and innocence. But where consciences are worried how to render God favorable, what they will reply, and with what assurance they will stand should they be called to his judgment, there we are not to reckon what the law requires, but Christ alone, who surpasses all perfection of the law, must be set forth as righteousness.

3.19.4–6   *(The second, freedom of conscience willingly obeying*
             without compulsion of the law)

3.19.4   *Freedom from the constraint of the law*
             establishes the true obedience of believers

The second part, dependent upon the first, is that consciences observe the law, not as if constrained by the necessity of the law, but that freed from the law's yoke they willingly obey God's will. For since they dwell in perpetual dread so long as they remain under the sway of the law, they will never be disposed with eager readiness to obey God unless they have already been given this sort of freedom.

3.19.5   *Freedom from constraint makes us capable of joyous obedience*

Those bound by the yoke of the law are like servants assigned certain tasks for each day by their masters. These servants think they have accomplished nothing, and dare not appear before their masters unless they have fulfilled the exact measure of their tasks. But sons, who are more generously and candidly treated by their fathers, do not hesitate to offer them incomplete and half-done and even defective works, trusting that their obedience and readiness of mind will be accepted by their fathers, even though they have not quite achieved what their fathers intended. Such children ought we to be, firmly trusting that our services will be approved by our most merciful Father, however small, rude, and imperfect these may be.

Emancipated by grace, believers need not fear the remnants of sin   3.19.6

(Freedom in "things indifferent" with proofs from Romans)   3.19.7–9

The third part of Christian freedom lies in this: regarding outward   3.19.7
things that are of themselves "indifferent," we are not bound before God by any religious obligation preventing us from sometimes using them and other times not using them, indifferently. And the knowledge of this freedom is very necessary for us, for if it is lacking, our consciences will have no repose and there will be no end to superstitions.

Freedom in the use of God's gifts for his purposes   3.19.8

We see whither this freedom tends: namely, that we should use God's gifts for the purpose for which he gave them to us, with no scruple of conscience, no trouble of mind. With such confidence our minds will be at peace with him, and will recognize his liberality toward us.

(Relation of Christian freedom to the weak and to the question of offenses)   3.19.10–13

On the right use of Christian freedom and the right renunciation of it   3.19.12

Nothing is plainer than this rule: that we should use our freedom if it results in the edification of our neighbor, but if it does not help our neighbor, then we should forgo it. . . . But it is the part of a godly man to realize that free power in outward matters has been given him in order that he may be the more ready for all the duties of love.

(Freedom and conscience in relation to traditions,   3.19.14–16
and to civil government)

The two kingdoms   3.19.15

Let us first consider that there is a twofold government in man: one aspect is spiritual, whereby the conscience is instructed in piety and in reverencing God; the second is political, whereby man is educated for the duties of humanity and citizenship that must be maintained among men.

Bondage and freedom of conscience

Therefore, as works have regard to men, so conscience refers to God. A good conscience, then, is nothing but inward integrity of heart.

PRAYER, WHICH IS THE CHIEF EXERCISE OF FAITH,
              AND BY WHICH WE DAILY RECEIVE GOD'S BENEFITS

(The nature and value of prayer)

Faith and prayer

The Lord willingly and freely reveals himself in his Christ. For in Christ he offers all happiness in place of our misery, all wealth in place of our neediness; in him he opens to us the heavenly treasures that our whole faith may contemplate his beloved Son, our whole expectation depend upon him, and our whole hope cleave to and rest in him. . . .

But after we have been instructed by faith to recognize that whatever we need and whatever we lack is in God, and in our Lord Jesus Christ, in whom the Father willed all the fullness of his bounty to abide [cf. Col. 1:19; John 1:16] so that we may all draw from it as from an overflowing spring, it remains for us to seek in him, and in prayers to ask of him, what we have learned to be in him.

The necessity of prayer

It is, therefore, by the benefit of prayer that we reach those riches which are laid up for us with the Heavenly Father. For there is a communion of men with God by which, having entered the heavenly sanctuary, they appeal to him in person concerning his promises in order to experience, where necessity so demands, that what they believed was not vain, although he had promised it in word alone. Therefore we see that to us nothing is promised to be expected from the Lord, which we are not also bidden to ask of him in prayers. So true is it that we dig up by prayer the treasures that were pointed out by the Lord's gospel, and which our faith has gazed upon.

Words fail to explain how necessary prayer is, and in how many ways the exercise of prayer is profitable. Surely, with good reason the

Heavenly Father affirms that the only stronghold of safety is in calling upon his name [cf. Joel 2:32]. By so doing we invoke the presence
both of his providence, through which he watches over and guards
our affairs, and of his power, through which he sustains us, weak as
we are and well-nigh overcome, and of his goodness, through which
he receives us, miserably burdened with sins, unto grace; and, in
short, it is by prayer that we call him to reveal himself as wholly present to us. Hence comes an extraordinary peace and repose to our consciences. For having disclosed to the Lord the necessity that was
pressing upon us, we even rest fully in the thought that none of our
ills is hid from him who, we are convinced, has both the will and the
power to take the best care of us.

(The rules of right prayer)   3.20.4–16

(First Rule: reverence)   3.20.4–5

(Second Rule: We pray from a sincere sense of want,   3.20.6–7
and with penitence)

(Third Rule: We yield all confidence in ourselves   3.20.8–10
and humbly plead for pardon)

The plea for forgiveness of sins as the most important part of prayer   3.20.9

The beginning, and even the preparation, of proper prayer is the plea
for pardon with a humble and sincere confession of guilt. . . .

   Even though the saints do not always beg forgiveness of sins in so
many words, if we diligently ponder their prayers that Scripture
relates, we shall readily come upon what I speak of: that they have
received their intention to pray from God's mercy alone, and thus
always have begun with appeasing him. For if anyone should question his own conscience, he would be so far from daring intimately to
lay aside his cares before God that, unless he relied upon mercy and
pardon, he would tremble at every approach.

(Fourth rule: We pray with confident hope)   3.20.11–14

Hope and faith overcome fear   3.20.11

The fourth rule is that, thus cast down and overcome by true humility, we should be nonetheless encouraged to pray by a sure hope that
our prayer will be answered. . . .

   For the saints the occasion that best stimulates them to call upon
God is when, distressed by their own need, they are troubled by the

greatest unrest, and are almost driven out of their senses, until faith opportunely comes to their relief. For among such tribulations God's goodness so shines upon them that even when they groan with weariness under the weight of present ills, and also are troubled and tormented by the fear of greater ones, yet, relying upon his goodness, they are relieved of the difficulty of bearing them, and are solaced and hope for escape and deliverance. . . . It is amazing how much our lack of trust provokes God if we request of him a boon that we do not expect.

(Prayer and faith)

It is faith that obtains whatever is granted to prayer. . . . God cannot be sincerely called upon by others than those to whom, through the preaching of the gospel, his kindness and gentle dealing have become known—indeed, have been intimately revealed.

3.20.12   *Against the denial of certainty that prayer is granted*

No one can well perceive the power of faith unless he feels it by experience in his heart. . . . If we would pray fruitfully, we ought therefore to grasp with both hands this assurance of obtaining what we ask, which the Lord enjoins with his own voice, and all the saints teach by their example. For only that prayer is acceptable to God which is born, if I may so express it, out of such presumption of faith, and is grounded in unshaken assurance of hope. . . . [P]rayers are vainly cast upon the air unless hope be added, from which we quietly watch for God as from a watchtower. . . .

Faith is not at all overthrown when it is joined with the acknowledgment of our misery, destitution, and uncleanness. For however much believers may feel pressed down or troubled by a heavy weight of sins, not only bereft of all things that might obtain favor with God, but laden with many offenses that justly render him terrifying, nevertheless they do not cease to present themselves; and this feeling does not frighten them from betaking themselves to him, since there is no other access to him. For prayer was not ordained that we should be haughtily puffed up before God, or greatly esteem anything of ours, but that, having confessed our guilt, we should deplore our distresses before him, as children unburden their troubles to their parents.

3.20.15–16   *(God hearkens even to defective prayers)*

3.20.16   *Our prayers can obtain an answer only through God's forgiveness*

What I have set forth on the four rules of right praying is not so rigorously required that God will reject those prayers in which he finds neither perfect faith nor repentance, together with a warmth of zeal and petitions rightly conceived. . . .

God tolerates even our stammering and pardons our ignorance whenever something inadvertently escapes us; as indeed without this mercy there would be no freedom to pray. . . . All prayers marred by these defects deserve to be repudiated; nevertheless, provided the saints bemoan their sins, chastise themselves, and immediately return to themselves, God pardons them.

There is no prayer which in justice God would not loathe if he did not overlook the spots with which all are sprinkled.

(The intercession of Christ)   3.20.17–20

Christ is the only Mediator,   3.20.19
even for the mutual intercession of believers

Now, since he is the only way, and the one access, by which it is granted us to come to God [cf. John 14:6], to those who turn aside from this way and forsake this access, no way and no access to God remain; nothing is left in his throne but wrath, judgment, and terror. . . . Christ is constituted the only Mediator, by whose intercession the Father is for us rendered gracious and easily entreated.

Christ does not by his intercession hinder us from pleading for one another by prayers in the church. So, then, let it remain an established principle that we should direct all intercessions of the whole church to that sole intercession. Indeed, especially for this reason should we beware of ungratefulness, because God, pardoning our unworthiness, not only allows individuals to pray for themselves but also permits men to plead for one another.

(Rejection of erroneous doctrines of the intercession of saints)   3.20.21–27

(Kinds of prayer: private and public)   3.20.28–30

Necessity and danger of public prayer   3.20.29

This constancy in prayer, even though it has especially to do with one's own private prayers, still is also concerned somewhat with the public prayers of the church. Yet these can neither be constant nor ought they even to take place otherwise than according to the polity agreed upon by common consent among all. This I grant you. For this reason, certain hours, indifferent to God but necessary for men's convenience, are agreed upon and appointed to provide for the accommodation of all, and for everything to be done "decently and in order" in the church, according to Paul's statement [I Cor. 14:40]. But this does not preclude each church from being both repeatedly stirred up to more frequent use of prayer and fired by a sharper zeal if it is alerted by some major need.

3.20.31–33   *(The use of singing, and of the spoken language)*

3.20.32   *Church singing*

Surely, if the singing be tempered to that gravity which is fitting in the sight of God and the angels, it both lends dignity and grace to sacred actions and has the greatest value in kindling our hearts to a true zeal and eagerness to pray. Yet we should be very careful that our ears be not more attentive to the melody than our minds to the spiritual meaning of the words.

3.20.34–42   *(The Lord's Prayer: exposition of the first three petitions)*

3.20.43   *The third petition*

3.20.44–47   *(Exposition of the last three petitions)*

3.20.48–49   *(Concluding considerations: adequacy of the Lord's Prayer, with freedom to use other words)*

3.20.50–52   *(Special times of prayer and undiscouraged perseverance in it)*

3.20.51   *Patient perseverance in prayer*

If, with minds composed to this obedience, we allow ourselves to be ruled by the laws of divine providence, we shall easily learn to persevere in prayer and, with desires suspended, patiently to wait for the Lord. Then we shall be sure that, even though he does not appear, he is always present to us, and will in his own time declare how he has never had ears deaf to the prayers that in men's eyes he seems to have neglected. This, then, will be an ever-present consolation: that, if God should not respond to our first requests, we may not faint or fall into despair. . . . Rather, by deferring our hope with a well-tempered evenness of mind, let us follow hard upon that perseverance which Scripture strongly commends to us.

3.20.52   *Unheard prayers?*

But if finally even after long waiting our senses cannot learn the benefit received from prayer, or perceive any fruit from it, still our faith will make us sure of what cannot be perceived by sense, that we have

obtained what was expedient. For the Lord so often and so certainly
promises to care for us in our troubles, when they have once been laid
upon his bosom. And so he will cause us to possess abundance in
poverty, and comfort in affliction. For though all things fail us, yet
God will never forsake us, who cannot disappoint the expectation
and patience of his people. He alone will be for us in place of all
things, since all good things are contained in him and he will reveal
them to us on the Day of Judgment, when his Kingdom will be plainly
manifested.

Besides, even if God grants our prayer, he does not always respond
to the exact form of our request but, seeming to hold us in suspense,
he yet, in a marvelous manner, shows us our prayers have not been
vain. . . . God, even when he does not comply with our wishes, is still
attentive and kindly to our prayers, so that hope relying upon his
word will never disappoint us. But believers need to be sustained by
this patience, since they would not long stand unless they relied upon
it. For the Lord proves his people by no light trials, and does not softly
exercise them, but often drives them to extremity, and allows them, so
driven, to lie a long time in the mire before he gives them any taste of
his sweetness. . . . Nevertheless, however they stand upon the assurance of that hope, they do not meanwhile cease to pray, for unless
there be in prayer a constancy to persevere, we pray in vain.

ETERNAL ELECTION, BY WHICH GOD HAS PREDESTINED   3.21
SOME TO SALVATION, OTHERS TO DESTRUCTION

(Importance of the doctrine of predestination   3.21.1–4
excludes both presumption and reticence in speaking of it)

Necessity and beneficial effect of the doctrine of election;   3.21.1
danger of curiosity

In actual fact, the covenant of life is not preached equally among all
men, and among those to whom it is preached, it does not gain the
same acceptance either constantly or in equal degree. In this diversity
the wonderful depth of God's judgment is made known. For there is
no doubt that this variety also serves the decision of God's eternal
election. If it is plain that it comes to pass by God's bidding that salvation is freely offered to some while others are barred from access to
it, at once great and difficult questions spring up, explicable only
when reverent minds regard as settled what they may suitably hold
concerning election and predestination. A baffling question this
seems to many. For they think nothing more inconsistent than that out

of the common multitude of men some should be predestined to salvation, others to destruction. . . . We shall never be clearly persuaded, as we ought to be, that our salvation flows from the wellspring of God's free mercy until we come to know his eternal election, which illumines God's grace by this contrast: that he does not indiscriminately adopt all into the hope of salvation but gives to some what he denies to others. . . .

Human curiosity renders the discussion of predestination, already somewhat difficult of itself, very confusing and even dangerous. No restraints can hold it back from wandering in forbidden bypaths and thrusting upward to the heights. If allowed, it will leave no secret to God that it will not search out and unravel. Since we see so many on all sides rushing into this audacity and impudence, among them certain men not otherwise bad, they should in due season be reminded of the measure of their duty in this regard.

First, then, let them remember that when they inquire into predestination they are penetrating the sacred precincts of divine wisdom. If anyone with carefree assurance breaks into this place, he will not succeed in satisfying his curiosity and he will enter a labyrinth from which he can find no exit. For it is not right for man unrestrainedly to search out things that the Lord has willed to be hid in himself, and to unfold from eternity itself the sublimest wisdom, which he would have us revere but not understand that through this also he should fill us with wonder. He has set forth by his Word the secrets of his will that he has decided to reveal to us. These he decided to reveal in so far as he foresaw that they would concern us and benefit us.

3.21.2 *Doctrine of predestination to be sought in Scripture only*

Let this, therefore, first of all be before our eyes: to seek any other knowledge of predestination than what the Word of God discloses is not less insane than if one should purpose to walk in a pathless waste [cf. Job 12:24], or to see in darkness. And let us not be ashamed to be ignorant of something in this matter, wherein there is a certain learned ignorance.

3.21.3 *The second danger: anxious silence about the doctrine of election*

There are others who, wishing to cure this evil, all but require that every mention of predestination be buried; indeed, they teach us to avoid any question of it, as we would a reef. . . . Therefore, to hold to a proper limit in this regard also, we shall have to turn back to the Word of the Lord, in which we have a sure rule for the understanding. For Scripture is the school of the Holy Spirit, in which, as nothing is omitted that is both necessary and useful to know, so nothing is taught but what is expedient to know. Therefore we must guard against depriving believers of anything disclosed about predestination in Scripture, lest we seem either wickedly to defraud them of the blessing of their God or to accuse and scoff at the Holy Spirit for having published what it is in any way profitable to suppress.

The alleged peril in the doctrine dismissed   3.21.4

We should not investigate what the Lord has left hidden in secret, that we should not neglect what he has brought into the open, so that we may not be convicted of excessive curiosity on the one hand, or of excessive ingratitude on the other.

(Predestination defined and explained   3.21.5–7
in relation to the Israelitish nation, and to individuals)

Predestination and foreknowledge of God; the election of Israel   3.21.5

No one who wishes to be thought religious dares simply deny predestination, by which God adopts some to hope of life, and sentences others to eternal death. But our opponents, especially those who make foreknowledge its cause, envelop it in numerous petty objections. We, indeed, place both doctrines in God, but we say that subjecting one to the other is absurd.

When we attribute foreknowledge to God, we mean that all things always were, and perpetually remain, under his eyes, so that to his knowledge there is nothing future or past, but all things are present. And they are present in such a way that he not only conceives them through ideas, as we have before us those things which our minds remember, but he truly looks upon them and discerns them as things placed before him. And this foreknowledge is extended throughout the universe to every creature. We call predestination God's eternal decree, by which he compacted with himself what he willed to become of each man. For all are not created in equal condition; rather, eternal life is foreordained for some, eternal damnation for others. Therefore, as any man has been created to one or the other of these ends, we speak of him as predestined to life or to death. God has attested this not only in individual persons but has given us an example of it in the whole offspring of Abraham, to make it clear that in his choice rests the future condition of each nation.

Confirmation of This Doctrine from Scriptural Testimonies

3.22.1–6   *(Election is not from foreknowledge of merit*
          but is of God's sovereign purpose)

3.22.1   *Election vs. foreknowledge of merits*

Many persons dispute all these positions which we have set forth, especially the free election of believers; nevertheless, this cannot be shaken. For generally these persons consider that God distinguishes among men according as he foresees what the merits of each will be. Therefore, he adopts as sons those whom he foreknows will not be unworthy of his grace; he appoints to the damnation of death those whose dispositions he discerns will be inclined to evil intention and ungodliness. . . . Because God chooses some, and passes over others according to his own decision, they bring an action against him. . . .

Now it behooves us to pay attention to what Scripture proclaims of every person. When Paul teaches that we were chosen in Christ "before the creation of the world" [Eph. 1:4a], he takes away all consideration of real worth on our part, for it is just as if he said: since among all the offspring of Adam, the Heavenly Father found nothing worthy of his election, he turned his eyes upon his Anointed, to choose from that body as members those whom he was to take into the fellowship of life. Let this reasoning, then, prevail among believers: we were adopted in Christ into the eternal inheritance because in ourselves we were not capable of such great excellence.

3.22.2   *Election before creation and not associated with foreknowledge of merit*

By saying that they were "elect before the creation of the world" [Eph. 1:4], he takes away all regard for worth. For what basis for distinction is there among those who did not yet exist, and who were subsequently to be equals in Adam? Now if they are elect in Christ, it follows that not only is each man elected without respect to his own person but also certain ones are separated from others, since we see that not all are members of Christ.

3.22.3   *Elected to be holy, not because already holy*

Wherever this decision of God's holds sway, there is no consideration of works. Of course, Paul does not develop the antithesis here, but it must be understood as he himself elsewhere explains it. "He called us," Paul says, "with a holy calling, not according to our works, but according to his own purpose, and the grace that was given to us by

Christ before time began" [II Tim. 1:9 p.]. And we have already shown
that in the words that follow, "that we should be holy and spotless"
[Eph. 1:4, cf. Vg.], we are freed of every doubt. Say: "Since he foresaw
that we would be holy, he chose us," and you will invert Paul's order.
Therefore you can safely infer the following: if he chose us that we
should be holy, he did not choose us because he foresaw that we
would be so. For these two notions disagree: that the godly have their
holiness from election, and that they arrive at election by reason of
works. The quibble to which they frequently have recourse, that the
Lord does not reward preceding merits with the grace of election yet
grants it to future merits, has no validity. For when it is said that
believers were chosen that they might be holy, at the same time it is
suggested that the holiness that was to be in them originated from
election.

(Answers to opponents of this basis of election,   3.22.7–11
which also is reprobation)

Rejection also takes place not on the basis of works   3.22.11
but solely according to God's will

"God has mercy upon whomever he wills, and he hardens whomever
he wills" [Rom. 9:18]. Do you see how Paul attributes both to God's
decision alone? If, then, we cannot determine a reason why he vouch-
safes mercy to his own, except that it so pleases him, neither shall we
have any reason for rejecting others, other than his will. For when it
is said that God hardens or shows mercy to whom he wills, men are
warned by this to seek no cause outside his will.

REFUTATION OF THE FALSE ACCUSATIONS WITH WHICH   3.23
THIS DOCTRINE HAS ALWAYS BEEN UNJUSTLY BURDENED

(Reprobation the concomitant of election and an act of God's will)   3.23.1–3

Election—but no reprobation?   3.23.1

Indeed many, as if they wished to avert a reproach from God, accept
election in such terms as to deny that anyone is condemned. But they
do this very ignorantly and childishly, since election itself could not
stand except as set over against reprobation. God is said to set apart
those whom he adopts into salvation; it will be highly absurd to say
that others acquire by chance or obtain by their own effort what election alone confers on a few. Therefore, those whom God passes over,

he condemns; and this he does for no other reason than that he wills to exclude them from the inheritance which he predestines for his own children. . . .

3.23.2–3   *(First objection: the doctrine of election makes God a tyrant)*

3.23.3   *God is just toward the reprobate*

If anyone approaches us with such expressions as: "Why from the beginning did God predestine some to death who, since they did not yet exist, could not yet have deserved the judgment of death?" let us, in lieu of reply, ask them, in turn, what they think God owes to man if He would judge him according to His own nature. As all of us are vitiated by sin, we can only be odious to God, and that not from tyrannical cruelty but by the fairest reckoning of justice. But if all whom the Lord predestines to death are by condition of nature subject to the judgment of death, of what injustice toward themselves may they complain?

3.23.4–7   *(God's justice not subject to our questioning)*

3.23.6   *Second objection: the doctrine of election*
             takes guilt and responsibility away from man

Since the disposition of all things is in God's hand, since the decision of salvation or of death rests in his power, he so ordains by his plan and will that among men some are born destined for certain death from the womb, who glorify his name by their own destruction. . . . If God only foresaw human events, and did not also dispose and determine them by his decision, then there would be some point in raising this question: whether his foreseeing had anything to do with their necessity. But since he foresees future events only by reason of the fact that he decreed that they take place, they vainly raise a quarrel over foreknowledge, when it is clear that all things take place rather by his determination and bidding.

3.23.7   *God has also predestined the fall into sin*

Whence does it happen that Adam's fall irremediably involved so many peoples, together with their infant offspring, in eternal death unless because it so pleased God? Here their tongues, otherwise so loquacious, must become mute. The decree is dreadful indeed, I confess. Yet no one can deny that God foreknew what end man was to have before he created him, and consequently foreknew because he so ordained by his decree.

(God willed, not only permitted, Adam's fall and the rejection of the reprobate, but with justice)   3.23.8–11

No distinction between God's will and God's permission   3.23.8

Here they have recourse to the distinction between will and permission. By this they would maintain that the wicked perish because God permits it, not because he so wills. But why shall we say "permission" unless it is because God so wills? Still, it is not in itself likely that man brought destruction upon himself through himself, by God's mere permission and without any ordaining. As if God did not establish the condition in which he wills the chief of his creatures to be! I shall not hesitate, then, simply to confess with Augustine that "the will of God is the necessity of things," and that what he has willed will of necessity come to pass, as those things which he has foreseen will truly come to pass.

Third objection: the doctrine of election leads to the view that God shows partiality toward persons   3.23.10

Do they ask how it happens that of two men indistinguishable in merit, God in his election passes over one but takes the other? I, in turn, ask: "Do they think that there is anything in him who is taken that disposes God to him?" If they admit that there is nothing, as they must, it will follow that God does not consider the man but seeks from his own goodness the reason to do him good. The fact that God therefore chooses one man but rejects another arises not out of regard to the man but solely from his mercy, which ought to be free to manifest and express itself where and when he pleases.

(Preaching of predestination not injurious but useful)   3.23.12–14

Fourth objection: the doctrine of election destroys all zeal for an upright life   3.23.12

Scripture does not speak of predestination with intent to rouse us to boldness that we may try with impious rashness to search out God's unattainable secrets. Rather, its intent is that, humbled and cast down, we may learn to tremble at his judgment and esteem his mercy. It is at this mark that believers aim. . . . Paul teaches that we have been chosen to this end: that we may lead a holy and blameless life [Eph. 1:4].

If election has as its goal holiness of life, it ought rather to arouse and goad us eagerly to set our mind upon it than to serve as a pretext for doing nothing. What a great difference there is between these two things: to cease well-doing because election is sufficient for salvation, and to devote ourselves to the pursuit of good as the appointed goal of election!

3.23.13   *Fifth objection: the doctrine of election*
          makes all admonitions meaningless

Christ commands us to believe in him. Yet when he says, "No one can come to me unless it has been granted him by my Father" [John 6:65], his statement is neither false nor contrary to his command. Let preaching, then, take its course that it may lead men to faith, and hold them fast in perseverance with continuing profit. And yet let not the knowledge of predestination be hindered, in order that those who obey may not be proud as of something of their own but may glory in the Lord. With reason, Christ says: "He who has ears to hear, let him hear" [Matt. 13:9].

3.24   ELECTION IS CONFIRMED BY GOD'S CALL;
          MOREOVER, THE WICKED BRING UPON THEMSELVES
          THE JUST DESTRUCTION TO WHICH THEY ARE DESTINED

3.24.1–5 *(The elect are effectually called,*
          and incorporated into the communion of Christ)

3.24.1   *The call is dependent upon election*
          and accordingly is solely a work of grace

Therefore, God designates as his children those whom he has chosen, and appoints himself their Father. Further, by calling, he receives them into his family and unites them to him so that they may together be one. But when the call is coupled with election, in this way Scripture sufficiently suggests that in it nothing but God's free mercy is to be sought. For if we ask whom he calls, and the reason why, he answers: whom he had chosen.

3.24.2   *The manner of the call itself clearly indicates*
          that it depends on grace alone

Even the very nature and dispensation of the call clearly demonstrate this fact, for it consists not only in the preaching of the Word but also in the illumination of the Spirit. . . . This inner call, then, is a pledge of salvation that cannot deceive us. To it applies John's statement: "We recognize that we are his children from the Spirit, which he has given us" [I John 3:24; cf. ch. 4:13].

Faith is the work of election,   3.24.3
but election does not depend upon faith

But here we must beware of two errors: for some make man God's co-worker, to ratify election by his consent. Thus, according to them, man's will is superior to God's plan. As if Scripture taught that we are merely given the ability to believe, and not, rather, faith itself! Others, although they do not so weaken the grace of the Holy Spirit yet led by some reason or other, make election depend upon faith, as if it were doubtful and also ineffectual until confirmed by faith. Indeed, that it is confirmed, with respect to us, is utterly plain; we have also already seen that the secret plan of God, which lay hidden, is brought to light, provided you understand by this language merely that what was unknown is now verified—sealed, as it were, with a seal. But it is false to say that election takes effect only after we have embraced the gospel, and takes its validity from this. We should indeed seek assurance of it from this; for if we try to penetrate to God's eternal ordination, that deep abyss will swallow us up. But when God has made plain his ordination to us, we must climb higher, lest the effect overwhelm the cause. For when Scripture teaches that we are illumined according as God has chosen us, what is more absurd and unworthy than for our eyes to be so dazzled by the brilliance of this light as to refuse to be mindful of election?

The right and wrong way to attain certainty of election   3.24.4

Therefore, as it is wrong to make the force of election contingent upon faith in the gospel, by which we feel that it appertains to us, so we shall be following the best order if, in seeking the certainty of our election, we cling to those latter signs which are sure attestations of it. . . .

Rare indeed is the mind that is not repeatedly struck with this thought: whence comes your salvation but from God's election? Now, what revelation do you have of your election? . . . Even though discussion about predestination is likened to a dangerous sea, still, in traversing it, one finds safe and calm—I also add pleasant—sailing unless he willfully desires to endanger himself. For just as those engulf themselves in a deadly abyss who, to make their election more certain, investigate God's eternal plan apart from his Word, so those who rightly and duly examine it as it is contained in his Word reap the inestimable fruit of comfort. Let this, therefore, be the way of our inquiry: to begin with God's call, and to end with it.

3.24.5   *Election is to be understood and recognized in Christ alone*

Now what is the purpose of election but that we, adopted as sons by our Heavenly Father, may obtain salvation and immortality by his favor? No matter how much you toss it about and mull it over, you will discover that its final bounds still extend no farther. Accordingly, those whom God has adopted as his sons are said to have been chosen not in themselves but in his Christ [Eph. 1:4]; for unless he could love them in him, he could not honor them with the inheritance of his Kingdom if they had not previously become partakers of him. But if we have been chosen in him, we shall not find assurance of our election in ourselves; and not even in God the Father, if we conceive him as severed from his Son. Christ, then, is the mirror wherein we must, and without self-deception may, contemplate our own election. For since it is into his body the Father has destined those to be engrafted whom he has willed from eternity to be his own, that he may hold as sons all whom he acknowledges to be among his members, we have a sufficiently clear and firm testimony that we have been inscribed in the book of life [cf. Rev. 21:27] if we are in communion with Christ.

3.24.6–11   *(Under Christ's protection the perseverance of the elect is secure: Scripture passages cited in objection interpreted)*

3.24.6   *Christ bestows upon his own the certainty that their election is irrevocable and lasting*

If we desire to know whether God cares for our salvation, let us inquire whether he has entrusted us to Christ, whom he has established as the sole Savior of all his people. If we still doubt whether we have been received by Christ into his care and protection, he meets that doubt when he willingly offers himself as shepherd, and declares that we shall be numbered among his flock if we hear his voice [John 10:3]. Let us therefore embrace Christ, who is graciously offered to us, and comes to meet us. He will reckon us in his flock and enclose us within his fold.

3.24.7   *He who truly believes cannot fall away*

Yet it daily happens that those who seemed to be Christ's fall away from him again, and hasten to destruction. Indeed, in that same passage, where he declares that none of those whom the Father had given to him perished, he nevertheless excepts the son of perdition [John 17:12]. True indeed, but it is also equally plain that such persons never cleaved to Christ with the heartfelt trust in which certainty of election has, I say, been established for us. "They went out from us," says John, "but they were not of us. For if they had been of us, they would no doubt have continued with us" [I John 2:19]. And I do not deny that they have signs of a call that are similar to those of the elect, but I by no means concede to them that sure establishment of election which I bid believers seek from the word of the gospel.

General and special calling [Matt. 22:2 ff.]   3.24.8

The statement of Christ "Many are called but few are chosen" [Matt. 22:14] is, in this manner, very badly understood. Nothing will be ambiguous if we hold fast to what ought to be clear from the foregoing: that there are two kinds of call. There is the general call, by which God invites all equally to himself through the outward preaching of the word—even those to whom he holds it out as a savor of death [cf. II Cor. 2:16], and as the occasion for severer condemnation. The other kind of call is special, which he deigns for the most part to give to the believers alone, while by the inward illumination of his Spirit he causes the preached Word to dwell in their hearts. Yet sometimes he also causes those whom he illumines only for a time to partake of it; then he justly forsakes them on account of their ungratefulness and strikes them with even greater blindness.

The elect before their call.   3.24.10
There is no "seed of election"

The elect are gathered into Christ's flock by a call not immediately at birth, and not all at the same time, but according as it pleases God to dispense his grace to them. But before they are gathered unto that supreme Shepherd, they wander scattered in the wilderness common to all; and they do not differ at all from others except that they are protected by God's especial mercy from rushing headlong into the final ruin of death. If you look upon them, you will see Adam's offspring, who savor of the common corruption of the mass. The fact that they are not carried to utter and even desperate impiety is not due to any innate goodness of theirs but because the eye of God watches over their safety and his hand is outstretched to them!

(How God deals with the reprobate)   3.24.12–17

THE FINAL RESURRECTION

3.25.1–4   *(Assertion of the doctrine of the final resurrection)*

3.25.1   *Importance of and hindrances to the resurrection hope*

He alone has fully profited in the gospel who has accustomed himself
to continual meditation upon the blessed resurrection.

3.25.3   *The resurrection hoped for is that of the body:*
           Christ's resurrection, the prototype

The very importance of the matter should sharpen our attention. For
Paul rightly argues that "if the dead do not rise up again, . . . the
whole gospel is vain and fallacious" [I Cor. 15:13–14 p.], for our condition would be more pitiable than that of all other mortals [I Cor.
15:19], seeing that, exposed to the hatred and reproach of many, we
are every hour in danger [cf. I Cor. 15:30], yea, "we are as sheep destined for the slaughter" [Rom. 8:36; Ps. 44:22; cf. v. 23, Comm.].
Accordingly, the authority of the gospel would fall not merely in one
part but in its entirety, which is embraced in our adoption and the
effecting of our salvation. Let us, then, be so attentive to this most
serious matter of all that no length of time may weary us. I have
deferred to this place my brief discussion of it for this purpose: that
my readers may learn, when they have received Christ, the Author of
perfect salvation, to rise up higher, and may know that he is clothed
in heavenly immortality and glory so that the whole body may be
conformed to the Head. Even thus in his person the Holy Spirit
repeatedly sets before us the example of the resurrection.

It is difficult to believe that bodies, when consumed with rotten-
ness, will at length be raised up in their season. Therefore, although
many of the philosophers declared souls immortal, few approved the
resurrection of the flesh. Even though there was no excuse for this
point of view, we are nevertheless reminded by it that it is something
too hard for men's minds to apprehend. Scripture provides two helps
by which faith may overcome this great obstacle: one in the parallel of
Christ's resurrection; the other in the omnipotence of God. . . .

Christ rose again that he might have us as companions in the life to
come. He was raised by the Father, inasmuch as he was Head of the
church, from which the Father in no way allows him to be severed. He
was raised by the power of the Holy Spirit, the Quickener of us in
common with him. Finally, he was raised that he might be "the resurrection and the life" [John 11:25].

(Objections of various classes of opponents to the doctrine refuted)   3.25.5–9

(Man's life in the hereafter: eternal enjoyment   3.25.10–12
of God's presence, or eternal misery in alienation from God)

Everlasting blessedness   3.25.10

But since the prophecy that death will be swallowed up in victory [Isa. 25:8; Hos. 13:14; I Cor. 15:54–55] will only then be fulfilled, let us always have in mind the eternal happiness, the goal of resurrection—a happiness of whose excellence the minutest part would scarce be told if all were said that the tongues of all men can say. . . . God contains the fullness of all good things in himself like an inexhaustible fountain, nothing beyond him is to be sought by those who strive after the highest good and all the elements of happiness. . . . If the Lord will share his glory, power, and righteousness with the elect—nay, will give himself to be enjoyed by them and, what is more excellent, will somehow make them to become one with himself, let us remember that every sort of happiness is included under this benefit. And although we have advanced considerably in this meditation, let us nevertheless acknowledge that, if our mental capacity be compared with the height of this mystery, we still remain at the very lowest roots. In this matter, we must all the more, then, keep sobriety, lest forgetful of our limitations we should soar aloft with the greater boldness, and be overcome by the brightness of the heavenly glory.

The lot of the reprobate   3.25.12

Now, because no description can deal adequately with the gravity of God's vengeance against the wicked, their torments and tortures are figuratively expressed to us by physical things, that is, by darkness, weeping, and gnashing of teeth [Matt. 8:12; 22:13], unquenchable fire [Matt. 3:12; Mark 9:43; Isa. 66:24], an undying worm gnawing at the heart [Isa. 66:24]. By such expressions the Holy Spirit certainly intended to confound all our senses with dread: as when he speaks of "a deep Gehenna prepared from eternity, fed with fire and much wood; the breath of the Lord, like a stream of brimstone, kindles it" [Isa. 30:33]. As by such details we should be enabled in some degree to conceive the lot of the wicked, so we ought especially to fix our thoughts upon this: how wretched it is to be cut off from all fellowship with God.

Book IV

The External Means or Aids by Which God Invites Us into the Society of Christ and Holds Us Therein

4.1 THE TRUE CHURCH WITH WHICH AS MOTHER
OF ALL THE GODLY WE MUST KEEP UNITY

4.1.1–4 *(The Holy Catholic Church, our mother)*

4.1.1 *The necessity of the church*

As explained in the previous book, it is by the faith in the gospel that Christ becomes ours and we are made partakers of the salvation and eternal blessedness brought by him. Since, however, in our ignorance and sloth (to which I add fickleness of disposition) we need outward helps to beget and increase faith within us, and advance it to its goal, God has also added these aids that he may provide for our weakness. And in order that the preaching of the gospel might flourish, he deposited this treasure in the church. He instituted "pastors and teachers" [Eph. 4:11] through whose lips he might teach his own; he furnished them with authority; finally, he omitted nothing that might make for holy agreement of faith and for right order. First of all, he instituted sacraments, which we who have experienced them feel to be highly useful aids to foster and strengthen faith. Shut up as we are in the prison house of our flesh, we have not yet attained angelic rank. God, therefore, in his wonderful providence accommodating himself to our capacity, has prescribed a way for us, though still far off, to draw near to him.

Accordingly, our plan of instruction now requires us to discuss the church, its government, orders, and power; then the sacraments; and lastly, the civil order.

What is the relationship of church and creed?

The article in the Creed in which we profess to "believe the church" refers not only to the visible church (our present topic) but also to all God's elect, in whose number are also included the dead. The word "believe" is used because often no other distinction can be made between God's children and the ungodly, between his own flock and wild beasts. There is no good reason why many insert the preposition "in." I admit that it is more usual and is not without the support of antiquity.... We testify that we believe *in* God because our mind reposes in him as truthful, and our trust rests in him. To say "*in* the church" would be as inappropriate as "*in* the forgiveness of sins" or "*in* the resurrection of the body." Consequently, although I do not wish to dispute over words, I should prefer to use the proper phrase, one better fitted to express the matter, rather than to affect forms of speaking which needlessly obscure it....

The church is called "catholic," or "universal," because there could not be two or three churches unless Christ be torn asunder [cf. I Cor. 1:13]—which cannot happen! But all the elect are so united in Christ [cf. Eph. 1:22–23] that as they are dependent on one Head, they also grow together into one body, being joined and knit together [cf. Eph. 4:16] as are the limbs of a body [Rom. 12:5; I Cor. 10:17; 12:12, 27]. They are made truly one since they live together in one faith, hope, and love, and in the same Spirit of God. For they have been called not only into the same inheritance of eternal life but also to participate in one God and Christ [Eph. 5:30].

"The communion of saints"

This article of the Creed also applies to some extent to the outward church, in that each of us should keep in brotherly agreement with all God's children, should yield to the church the authority it deserves, in short, should act as one of the flock. Accordingly, "the communion of saints" is added. This clause, though generally omitted by the ancients, ought not to be overlooked, for it very well expresses what the church is. It is as if one said that the saints are gathered into the society of Christ on the principle that whatever benefits God confers upon them, they should in turn share with one another....

Now, it is very important for us to know what benefit we shall gain from this. The basis on which we believe the church is that we are fully convinced we are members of it. In this way our salvation rests upon sure and firm supports, so that, even if the whole fabric of the world were overthrown, the church could neither totter nor fall. First, it stands by God's election, and cannot waver or fail any more than his eternal providence can. Secondly, it has in a way been joined to the steadfastness of Christ, who will no more allow his believers to be estranged from him than that his members be rent and torn asunder. Besides, we are certain that, while we remain within the bosom of the church, the truth will always abide with us. Finally, we feel that these promises apply to us: "There will be salvation in Zion" [Joel 2:32; Obad. 17, cf. Vg.]; "God will abide in the midst of Jerusalem forever, that it may never be moved" [Ps. 46:5]. So powerful is participation in the church that it keeps us in the society of God. In the very word "communion" there is a wealth of comfort because, while it is determined that whatever the Lord bestows upon his members and ours belongs to us, our hope is strengthened by all the benefits they receive.

Yet, to embrace the unity of the church in this way, we need not (as we have said) see the church with the eyes or touch it with the hands. Rather, the fact that it belongs to the realm of faith should warn us to regard it no less since it passes our understanding than if it were clearly visible. And our faith is no worse because it recognizes a church beyond our ken. For here we are not bidden to distinguish between reprobate and elect—that is for God alone, not for us, to do—but to establish with certainty in our hearts that all those who, by the kindness of God the Father, through the working of the Holy Spirit, have entered into fellowship with Christ, are set apart as God's property and personal possession; and that when we are of their number we share that great grace.

4.1.4 *The visible church as mother of believers*

But because it is now our intention to discuss the visible church, let us learn even from the simple title "mother" how useful, indeed how necessary, it is that we should know her. For there is no other way to enter into life unless this mother conceive us in her womb, give us birth, nourish us at her breast, and lastly, unless she keep us under her care and guidance until, putting off mortal flesh, we become like the angels [Matt. 22:30]. Our weakness does not allow us to be dismissed from her school until we have been pupils all our lives. Furthermore, away from her bosom one cannot hope for any forgiveness of sins or any salvation, as Isaiah [Isa. 37:32] and Joel [Joel 2:32] testify.

(Her ministers, speaking for God, not to be despised)   4.1.5–6

Education through the church, its value and its obligation   4.1.5

But let us proceed to set forth what pertains to this topic. Paul writes that Christ, "that he might fill all things," appointed some to be "apostles, some prophets, some evangelists, some pastors and teachers, for the equipment of the saints, for the work of the ministry, for the building up of the body of Christ, until we all reach the unity of the faith and of the knowledge of the Son of God, to perfect manhood, to the measure of the fully mature age of Christ" [Eph. 4:10–13, Comm., but cf. also Vg.]. We see how God, who could in a moment perfect his own, nevertheless desires them to grow up into manhood solely under the education of the church. We see the way set for it: the preaching of the heavenly doctrine has been enjoined upon the pastors. We see that all are brought under the same regulation, that with a gentle and teachable spirit they may allow themselves to be governed by teachers appointed to this function. . . .

As he was of old not content with the law alone, but added priests as interpreters from whose lips the people might ask its true meaning [cf. Mal. 2:7], so today he not only desires us to be attentive to its reading, but also appoints instructors to help us by their effort. This is doubly useful. On the one hand, he proves our obedience by a very good test when we hear his ministers speaking just as if he himself spoke. On the other, he also provides for our weakness in that he prefers to address us in human fashion through interpreters in order to draw us to himself, rather than to thunder at us and drive us away. Indeed, from the dread with which God's majesty justly overwhelms them, all the pious truly feel how much this familiar sort of teaching is needed. . . .

Those who think the authority of the Word is dragged down by the baseness of the men called to teach it disclose their own ungratefulness. For, among the many excellent gifts with which God has adorned the human race, it is a singular privilege that he deigns to consecrate to himself the mouths and tongues of men in order that his voice may resound in them.

(The visible church: its membership   4.1.7–9
and the marks by which it is recognized)

Invisible and visible church   4.1.7

Holy Scripture speaks of the church in two ways. Sometimes by the term "church" it means that which is actually in God's presence, into which no persons are received but those who are children of God by grace of adoption and true members of Christ by sanctification of the Holy Spirit. Then, indeed, the church includes not only the saints presently living on earth, but all the elect from the beginning of the world. Often, however, the name "church" designates the whole multitude of men spread over the earth who profess to worship one God and Christ. By baptism we are initiated into faith in him; by partaking in the Lord's Supper we attest our unity in true doctrine and love; in the Word of the Lord we have agreement, and for the preaching of the Word the ministry instituted by Christ is preserved. In this church are mingled many hypocrites who have nothing of Christ but the name and outward appearance. There are very many ambitious, greedy, envious persons, evil speakers, and some of quite unclean life. Such are tolerated for a time either because they cannot be convicted by a competent tribunal or because a vigorous discipline does not always flourish as it ought.

Just as we must believe, therefore, that the former church, invisible to us, is visible to the eyes of God alone, so we are commanded to revere and keep communion with the latter, which is called "church" in respect to men.

4.1.8 *The limitation of our judgment*

Accordingly, the Lord by certain marks and tokens has pointed out to us what we should know about the church. As we have cited above from Paul, to know who are His is a prerogative belonging solely to God [II Tim. 2:19]. Steps were indeed thus taken to restrain men's undue rashness; and daily events themselves remind us how far his secret judgments surpass our comprehension. For those who seemed utterly lost and quite beyond hope are by his goodness called back to the way; while those who more than others seemed to stand firm often fall. Therefore, according to God's secret predestination (as Augustine says), "many sheep are without, and many wolves are within." For he knows and has marked those who know neither him nor themselves. Of those who openly wear his badge, his eyes alone see the ones who are unfeignedly holy and will persevere to the very end [Matt. 24:13]—the ultimate point of salvation.

But on the other hand, because he foresaw it to be of some value for us to know who were to be counted as his children, he has in this regard accommodated himself to our capacity. And, since assurance of faith was not necessary, he substituted for it a certain charitable judgment whereby we recognize as members of the church those who, by confession of faith, by example of life, and by partaking of the sacraments, profess the same God and Christ with us.

He has, moreover, set off by plainer marks the knowledge of his very body to us, knowing how necessary it is to our salvation.

The marks of the church and our application of them to judgment   4.1.9

From this the face of the church comes forth and becomes visible to our eyes. Wherever we see the Word of God purely preached and heard, and the sacraments administered according to Christ's institution, there, it is not to be doubted, a church of God exists [cf. Eph. 2:20]. For his promise cannot fail: "Wherever two or three are gathered in my name, there I am in the midst of them" [Matt. 18:20].

But that we may clearly grasp the sum of this matter, we must proceed by the following steps: the church universal is a multitude gathered from all nations; it is divided and dispersed in separate places, but agrees on the one truth of divine doctrine, and is bound by the bond of the same religion. Under it are thus included individual churches, disposed in towns and villages according to human need, so that each rightly has the name and authority of the church. Individual men who, by their profession of religion, are reckoned within such churches, even though they may actually be strangers to the church, still in a sense belong to it until they have been rejected by public judgment.

(A church with these marks, however defective,   4.1.10–16
is not to be forsaken: the sin of schism)

The false claim of perfection comes from distorted opinion   4.1.16

Because God willed that the communion of his church be maintained in this outward society, he who out of hatred of the wicked breaks the token of that society treads a path that slopes to a fall from the communion of saints.

Let them ponder that in a great multitude there are many men, truly holy and innocent in the Lord's sight, who escape their notice. Let them ponder that even among those who seem diseased there are many who in no wise are pleased with, or flatter themselves in, their faults, but aroused again and again by a profound fear of the Lord, aspire to a more upright life. Let them ponder that a man is not to be judged for one deed, inasmuch as the holiest sometimes undergo a most grievous fall. Let them ponder how much more important both the ministry of the Word and participation in the sacred mysteries are for the gathering of the church than the possibility that this whole power may be dissipated through the guilt of certain ungodly men. Finally, let them realize that in estimating the true church divine judgment is of more weight than human.

4.1.17–22 *(The imperfect holiness of the church does not justify schism, but affords occasion for the exercise within it of the forgiveness of sins)*

4.1.17 *The holiness of the church*

Because they also allege that the church is not without basis called holy, it is fitting to examine in what holiness it excels lest, if we are not willing to admit a church unless it be perfect in every respect, we leave no church at all. True, indeed, is Paul's statement: "Christ . . . gave himself up for the church that he might sanctify her; he cleansed her by the washing of water in the word of life, that he might present her to himself as his glorious bride, without spot or wrinkle," etc. [Eph. 5:25–27 p.]. Yet it also is no less true that the Lord is daily at work in smoothing out wrinkles and cleansing spots. From this it follows that the church's holiness is not yet complete. The church is holy, then, in the sense that it is daily advancing and is not yet perfect: it makes progress from day to day but has not yet reached its goal of holiness.

4.1.19 *The example of Christ and of the apostles*

Let the following two points, then, stand firm. First, he who voluntarily deserts the outward communion of the church (where the Word of God is preached and the sacraments are administered) is without excuse. Secondly, neither the vices of the few nor the vices of the many in any way prevent us from duly professing our faith there in ceremonies ordained by God. For a godly conscience is not wounded by the unworthiness of another, whether pastor or layman; nor are the sacraments less pure and salutary for a holy and upright man because they are handled by unclean persons.

4.1.20 *Forgiveness of sins and the church*

In the Creed forgiveness of sins appropriately follows mention of the church. . . . Forgiveness of sins, then, is for us the first entry into the church and Kingdom of God. Without it, there is for us no covenant or bond with God. . . . [W]e are initiated into the society of the church by the sign of baptism, which teaches us that entrance into God's family is not open to us unless we first are cleansed of our filth by his goodness.

4.1.21 *Lasting forgiveness for the members of the church!*

Not only does the Lord through forgiveness of sins receive and adopt us once for all into the church, but through the same means he preserves and protects us there. For what would be the point of providing a pardon for us that was destined to be of no use? Every godly man is his own witness that the Lord's mercy, if it were granted only once, would be void and illusory, since each is quite aware throughout his life of the many infirmities that need God's mercy. And clearly not in vain does God promise this grace especially to those of his own household; not in vain does he order the same message of reconciliation daily to be brought to them. So, carrying, as we do, the traces of sin around with us throughout life, unless we are sustained by the Lord's constant grace in forgiving our sins, we shall scarcely abide one moment in the church. But the Lord has called his children to eternal salvation. Therefore, they ought to ponder that there is pardon ever ready for their sins. Consequently, we must firmly believe that by God's generosity, mediated by Christ's merit, through the sanctification of the Spirit, sins have been and are daily pardoned to us who have been received and engrafted into the body of the church.

The power of the keys   4.1.22

We should accordingly note three things here. First, however great the holiness in which God's children excel, they still—so long as they dwell in mortal bodies—remain unable to stand before God without forgiveness of sins. Secondly, this benefit so belongs to the church that we cannot enjoy it unless we abide in communion with the church. Thirdly, it is dispensed to us through the ministers and pastors of the church, either by the preaching of the gospel or by the administration of the sacraments; and herein chiefly stands out the power of the keys, which the Lord has conferred upon the society of believers. Accordingly, let each one of us count it his own duty to seek forgiveness of sins only where the Lord has placed it.

(Incidents illustrating forgiveness within the community of believers)   4.1.23–29

A COMPARISON OF THE FALSE AND THE TRUE CHURCH   4.2

(Departure from true doctrine and worship invalidates   4.2.1–6
the Roman Church's claim to be the true church)

(The Roman Church compared with ancient Israel   4.2.7–11
as to worship and jurisdiction)

The sound elements do not make the corrupted church a true church   4.2.12

4.3					THE DOCTORS AND MINISTERS OF THE CHURCH,
					THEIR ELECTION AND OFFICE

4.3.1–3	*(The ministry given by God: its high and necessary functions)*

4.3.1	*Why does God need men's service?*

Now we must speak of the order by which the Lord willed his church
to be governed. He alone should rule and reign in the church as well
as have authority or pre-eminence in it, and this authority should be
exercised and administered by his Word alone. Nevertheless, because
he does not dwell among us in visible presence [Matt. 26:11], we have
said that he uses the ministry of men to declare openly his will to us
by mouth, as a sort of delegated work, not by transferring to them his
right and honor, but only that through their mouths he may do his
own work—just as a workman uses a tool to do his work. . . .

This is the best and most useful exercise in humility, when he
accustoms us to obey his Word, even though it be preached through
men like us and sometimes even by those of lower worth than we. If
he spoke from heaven, it would not be surprising if his sacred oracles
were to be reverently received without delay by the ears and minds
of all. For who would not dread the presence of his power? Who
would not be stricken down at the sight of such great majesty? Who
would not be confounded at such boundless splendor? But when a
puny man risen from the dust speaks in God's name, at this point we
best evidence our piety and obedience toward God if we show ourselves teachable toward his minister, although he excels us in nothing.
It was for this reason, then, that he hid the treasure of his heavenly
wisdom in weak and earthen vessels [II Cor. 4:7] in order to prove
more surely how much we should esteem it.

4.3.2	*The significance of the ministry for the church*

This human ministry which God uses to govern the church is the chief
sinew by which believers are held together in one body. . . . For neither the light and heat of the sun, nor food and drink, are so necessary
to nourish and sustain the present life as the apostolic and pastoral
office is necessary to preserve the church on earth.

4.3.4–9	*(The Scriptural offices of the ministry described)*

4.3.4	*The several sorts of officers according to Eph., ch. 4*

Those who preside over the government of the church in accordance
with Christ's institution are called by Paul as follows: first apostles,

then prophets, thirdly evangelists, fourthly pastors, and finally teachers [Eph. 4:11]. Of these only the last two have an ordinary office in the church; the Lord raised up the first three at the beginning of his Kingdom, and now and again revives them as the need of the times demands.

Temporary and permanent offices   4.3.5

We have now in mind which ministries in the government of the church were temporary and which ones were so instituted as to endure permanently. But if we group evangelists and apostles together, we shall then have two pairs that somehow correspond with each other. For as our teachers correspond to the ancient prophets, so do our pastors to the apostles.

The designation of ministers of the Word: presbyters   4.3.8

But in indiscriminately calling those who rule the church "bishops," "presbyters," "pastors," and "ministers," I did so according to Scriptural usage, which interchanges these terms. . . .

Governors [I Cor. 12:28] were, I believe, elders chosen from the people, who were charged with the censure of morals and the exercise of discipline along with the bishops. For one cannot otherwise interpret his statement, "Let him who rules act with diligence" [Rom. 12:8, cf. Vg.]. Each church, therefore, had from its beginning a senate, chosen from godly, grave, and holy men, which had jurisdiction over the correcting of faults. . . . Experience itself makes clear that this sort of order was not confined to one age. Therefore, this office of government is necessary for all ages.

The deacons   4.3.9

The care of the poor was entrusted to the deacons. However, two kinds are mentioned in the letter to the Romans: "He that gives, let him do it with simplicity; . . . he that shows mercy, with cheerfulness [Rom. 12:8, cf. Vg.]. Since it is certain that Paul is speaking of the public office of the church, there must have been two distinct grades. Unless my judgment deceive me, in the first clause he designates the deacons who distribute the alms. But the second refers to those who had devoted themselves to the care of the poor and sick. Of this sort were the widows whom Paul mentions to Timothy [I Tim. 5:9–10].

(The calling, authorization, and ordination of ministers)   4.3.10–16

4.3.10   *Orderly calling is requisite*

But while "all things should be done decently and in order" [I Cor.
14:40] in the holy assembly, there is nothing in which order should be
more diligently observed than in establishing government; for
nowhere is there greater peril if anything be done irregularly. Therefore, in order that noisy and troublesome men should not rashly take
upon themselves to teach or to rule (which might otherwise happen),
especial care was taken that no one should assume public office in the
church without being called. Therefore, if a man were to be considered a true minister of the church, he must first have been duly called
[Heb. 5:4], then he must respond to his calling, that is, he must undertake and carry out the tasks enjoined.

4.3.11   *Outer and inner call*

The treatment of this matter involves four points: that we may know
(1) what sort of ministers they should be, (2) how, and (3) by whom
they should be appointed, and (4) by what rite or ceremony they
should be installed. I am speaking of the outward and solemn call
which has to do with the public order of the church. I pass over that
secret call, of which each minister is conscious before God, and which
does not have the church as witness.

4.3.12   *Who can become a minister of the church? How this takes place*

In two passages [Titus 1:7; I Tim. 3:1–7] Paul fully sets forth what sort
of bishops ought to be chosen. To sum up, only those are to be chosen
who are of sound doctrine and of holy life, not notorious in any fault
which might both deprive them of authority and disgrace the ministry [I Tim. 3:2–3; Titus 1:7–8].

4.3.13   *Who should choose ministers?*

The third point in our discussion is: who should choose the ministers?
The election of the apostles provides no sure rule in this matter, for it
was somewhat different from the calling of the rest.

4.3.15   *The vote of the people*

Someone now asks whether the minister ought to be chosen by the
whole church, or only by his colleagues and the elders charged with
the censure of morals, or whether he ought to be appointed by the
authority of a single person.

We therefore hold that this call of a minister is lawful according to the Word of God, when those who seemed fit are created by the consent and approval of the people; moreover, that other pastors ought to preside over the election in order that the multitude may not go wrong either through fickleness, through evil intentions, or through disorder.

Ordination 4.3.16

There remains the rite of ordination, to which we have given the last place in the call. It is clear that when the apostles admitted any man to the ministry, they used no other ceremony than the laying on of hands, I judge that this rite derived from the custom of the Hebrews, who, as it were, presented to God by the laying on of hands that which they wished to be blessed and consecrated.

THE CONDITION OF THE ANCIENT CHURCH, 4.4
AND THE KIND OF GOVERNMENT IN USE BEFORE THE PAPACY

(Historical development of the ministry; three classes of ministers: 4.4.1–4
teaching and ruling presbyters: one presbyter selected to be bishop:
the archbishop)

(Deacons and archdeacons: the administration 4.4.5–9
of property and alms: minor clerics)

(History of changes in the election and ordination of ministers: 4.4.10–15
consent of the magistrates, clergy, and people in the election of bishops)

THE ANCIENT FORM OF GOVERNMENT WAS 4.5
COMPLETELY OVERTHROWN BY THE TYRANNY OF THE PAPACY

(Appointment of unqualified persons without vote of the people) 4.5.1–3

(Abuses associated with collation to clerical benefices) 4.5.4–7

(Negligence and idleness of monks, canons, 4.5.8–10
and others holding clerical office)

(Corruption and covetousness prevail 4.5.11–19
in the ranks of bishops, pastors, and deacons)

4.8.1   *Task and limits of the church's doctrinal authority*

The power of the church . . . resides partly in individual bishops, and partly in councils, either provincial or general. I speak only of the spiritual power, which is proper to the church. This, moreover, consists either in doctrine or in jurisdiction or in making laws. The doctrinal side has two parts: authority to lay down articles of faith, and authority to explain them . . .

The power of the church is therefore to be not grudgingly manifested but yet to be kept within definite limits, that it may not be drawn hither and thither according to men's whim.

The doctrinal authority of Moses and the priests   4.8.2

Accordingly, we must here remember that whatever authority and dignity the Spirit in Scripture accords to either priests or prophets, or apostles, or successors of apostles, it is wholly given not to the men personally, but to the ministry to which they have been appointed; or (to speak more briefly) to the Word, whose ministry is entrusted to them. For if we examine them all in order, we shall not find that they have been endowed with any authority to teach or to answer, except in the name and Word of the Lord. For, where they are called to office, it is at the same time enjoined upon them not to bring anything of themselves, but to speak from the Lord's mouth. And he himself does not bring them forth to be heard by the people before teaching them what to speak: they are to speak nothing but his Word.

The doctrinal authority of the apostles   4.8.4

The power of the church, therefore, is not infinite but subject to the Lord's Word and, as it were, enclosed within it.

Scriptural foundation of the Word of God in the Old Covenant   4.8.6

But where it pleased God to raise up a more visible form of the church, he willed to have his Word set down and sealed in writing, that his priests might seek from it what to teach the people, and that every doctrine to be taught should conform to that rule. Therefore, after the law has been published, the priests are bidden to teach "from the mouth of the Lord" [Mal. 2:7, cf. Vg. and Comm.]. This means that they should teach nothing strange or foreign to that doctrine which God included in the law; indeed, it was unlawful for them to add to it or take away from it [Deut. 4:2; 13:1].

There then followed the prophets, through whom God published new oracles which were added to the law—but not so new that they did not flow from the law and hark back to it. As for doctrine, they were only interpreters of the law and added nothing to it except predictions of things to come. Apart from these, they brought nothing forth but a pure exposition of the law. But because the Lord was pleased to reveal a clearer and fuller doctrine in order better to satisfy weak consciences, he commanded that the prophecies also be committed to writing and be accounted part of his Word. At the same time, histories were added to these, also the labor of the prophets, but composed under the Holy Spirit's dictation. I include the psalms with the prophecies, since what we attribute to the prophecies is common to them.

Therefore, that whole body, put together out of law, prophecies, psalms, and histories, was the Lord's Word for the ancient people; and to this standard, priests and teachers, even to the coming of Christ, had to conform their teaching. And it was not lawful for them to turn aside either to the right or to the left [Deut. 5:32], for their whole office was limited to answering the people from the mouth of God.

4.8.8   *The apostles authorized to teach what Christ commanded*

Let this be a firm principle: No other word is to be held as the Word of God, and given place as such in the church, than what is contained first in the Law and the Prophets, then in the writings of the apostles; and the only authorized way of teaching in the church is by the prescription and standard of his Word.

4.8.10–16   *(Rejection of claims of doctrinal infallibility apart from the Word)*

4.9   COUNCILS AND THEIR AUTHORITY

4.9.1–2   *(True authority of church councils)*

4.9.3–7   *(Defects of pastors render their councils fallible)*

4.9.8–11   *(Departing from Scripture, councils have deteriorated,
             but even those of Nicaea and Chalcedon were defective)*

4.9.12–14   *(We must not obey blind guides;
              decisions of later councils faulty in the light of Scripture)*

4.10   THE POWER OF MAKING LAWS, IN WHICH THE POPE,
                 WITH HIS SUPPORTERS, HAS EXERCISED UPON SOULS
                      THE MOST SAVAGE TYRANNY AND BUTCHERY

4.10.1–4   *(Church laws and traditions, and the Christian's conscience before God)*

4.10.5–8   *(Conscience in relation to human and papal laws: God the only lawgiver)*

4.10.9–18   *(Ecclesiastical constitutions authorizing ceremonies in worship are
              tyrannous, frivolous, and contrary to Scripture)*

Necessity of church constitutions   4.10.27

First, let us grasp this consideration. We see that some form of organization is necessary in all human society to foster the common peace
and maintain concord. We further see that in human transactions
some procedure is always in effect, which is to be respected in the
interests of public decency, and even of humanity itself. This ought
especially to be observed in churches, which are best sustained when
all things are under a well-ordered constitution, and which without
concord become no churches at all. Therefore, if we wish to provide
for the safety of the church, we must attend with all diligence to
Paul's command that "all things be done decently and in order"
[I Cor. 14:40].

Yet since such diversity exists in the customs of men, such variety
in their minds, such conflicts in their judgments and dispositions, no
organization is sufficiently strong unless constituted with definite
laws; nor can any procedure be maintained without some set form.
Therefore, we are so far from condemning the laws that conduce to
this as to contend that, when churches are deprived of them, their
very sinews disintegrate and they are wholly deformed and scattered.
Nor can Paul's requirement—that "all things be done decently and in
order"—be met unless order itself and decorum be established
through the addition of observances that form, as it were, a bond of
union.

But in these observances one thing must be guarded against. They
are not to be considered necessary for salvation and thus bind consciences by scruples; nor are they to be associated with the worship of
God, and piety thus be lodged in them.

The problem of right church constitutions   4.10.28

But it is worth-while to define still more clearly what is included
under that decorum which Paul commends, and also under order
[I Cor. 14:40].

The purpose of decorum is in part that, when rites are used which promote reverence toward sacred things, we be aroused to piety by such aids; in part, also, that modesty and gravity, which ought to be seen in all honorable acts, may greatly shine there. The first point in order is that those in charge know the rule and law of good governing, but that the people who are governed become accustomed to obedience to God and to right discipline. The second point is, when we have the church set up in good order, we provide for its peace and quietness.

4.10.30   *Bondage and freedom of church constitutions*

I approve only those human constitutions which are founded upon God's authority, drawn from Scripture, and, therefore, wholly divine. Let us take, for example, kneeling when solemn prayers are being said. The question is whether it is a human tradition, which any man may lawfully repudiate or neglect. I say that it is human, as it is also divine. It is of God in so far as it is a part of that decorum whose care and observance the apostle has commended to us [I Cor. 14:40]. But it is of men in so far as it specifically designates what had in general been suggested rather than explicitly stated.

By this one example we may judge what opinion we should have of this whole class. I mean that the Lord has in his sacred oracles faithfully embraced and clearly expressed both the whole sum of true righteousness, and all aspects of the worship of his majesty, and whatever was necessary to salvation; therefore, in these the Master alone is to be heard. But because he did not will in outward discipline and ceremonies to prescribe in detail what we ought to do (because he foresaw that this depended upon the state of the times, and he did not deem one form suitable for all ages), here we must take refuge in those general rules which he has given, that whatever the necessity of the church will require for order and decorum should be tested against these. Lastly, because he has taught nothing specifically, and because these things are not necessary to salvation, and for the upbuilding of the church ought to be variously accommodated to the customs of each nation and age, it will be fitting (as the advantage of the church will require) to change and abrogate traditional practices and to establish new ones. Indeed, I admit that we ought not to charge into innovation rashly, suddenly, for insufficient cause. But love will best judge what may hurt or edify; and if we let love be our guide, all will be safe.

4.10.31   *Bondage and freedom over against church constitutions*

What sort of freedom of conscience could there be in such excessive attentiveness and caution? Indeed, it will be very clear when we consider that these are no fixed and permanent sanctions by which we are bound, but outward rudiments for human weakness. Although not all of us need them, we all use them, for we are mutually bound, one to another, to nourish mutual love. This may be recognized in the examples set forth above. What? Does religion consist in a woman's shawl, so that it is unlawful for her to go out with a bare head? Is that decree of Paul's concerning silence so holy that it cannot be broken without great offense? Is there in bending the knee or in burying a corpse any holy rite that cannot be neglected without offense? Not at all. For if a woman needs such haste to help a neighbor that she cannot stop to cover her head, she does not offend if she runs to her with head uncovered. And there is a place where it is no less proper for her to speak than elsewhere to remain silent. Also, nothing prohibits a man who cannot bend his knees because of disease from standing to pray. Finally, it is better to bury a dead man in due time than, where a shroud is lacking, or where there are no pallbearers to carry him, to wait until the unburied corpse decays. Nevertheless, the established custom of the region, or humanity itself and the rule of modesty, dictate what is to be done or avoided in these matters. In them a man commits no crime if out of imprudence or forgetfulness he departs from them; but if out of contempt, this willfulness is to be disapproved. Similarly, the days themselves, the hours, the structure of the places of worship, what psalms are to be sung on what day, are matters of no importance. But it is convenient to have definite days and stated hours, and a place suitable to receive all, if there is any concern for the preservation of peace.

THE JURISDICTION OF THE CHURCH AND ITS ABUSE AS SEEN IN THE PAPACY

4.11

(Jurisdiction and discipline: the power of the keys and the civil magistracy)

4.11.1–5

The basis of church jurisdiction in the power of the keys

4.11.1

There remains the third part of ecclesiastical power, the most important in a well-ordered state. This, as we have said, consists in jurisdiction. . . . For as no city or township can function without magistrate and polity, so the church of God (as I have already taught, but am now compelled to repeat) needs a spiritual polity. This is, however, quite distinct from the civil polity, yet does not hinder or threaten it but rather greatly helps and furthers it. Therefore, this power of jurisdiction will be nothing, in short, but an order framed for the preservation of the spiritual polity.

For this purpose courts of judgment were established in the church from the beginning to deal with the censure of morals, to investigate vices, and to be charged with the exercise of the office of the keys. Paul designates this order in his letter to the Corinthians when he mentions offices of ruling [I Cor. 12:28].

4.11.3   *Civil and ecclesiastical jurisdiction*

The church does not have the right of the sword to punish or compel, not the authority to force; not imprisonment, nor the other punishments which the magistrate commonly inflicts. Then, it is not a question of punishing the sinner against his will, but of the sinner professing his repentance in a voluntary chastisement. The two conceptions are very different. The church does not assume what is proper to the magistrate; nor can the magistrate execute what is carried out by the church. . . . [A]s the magistrate ought by punishment and physical restraint to cleanse the church of offenses, so the minister of the Word in turn ought to help the magistrate in order that not so many may sin. Their functions ought to be so joined that each serves to help, not hinder, the other.

4.11.6–10   *(Abuses caused by the unwarranted assumption of power by the bishops)*

4.11.11–16   *(Inordinate and fraudulent claims of the papacy*
and its usurpation of worldly powers)

4.12   THE DISCIPLINE OF THE CHURCH:
ITS CHIEF USE IN CENSURES AND EXCOMMUNICATION

4.12.1–7   *(Discussion of power of the keys in true discipline:*
the ends and processes of discipline)

4.12.1   *Necessity and nature of church discipline*

Discipline depends for the most part upon the power of the keys and upon spiritual jurisdiction. To understand it better, let us divide the church into two chief orders: clergy and people. I call by the usual name "clergy" those who perform the public ministry in the church. We shall first speak of common discipline, to which all ought to submit; then we shall come to the clergy, who, besides the common discipline, have their own.

But because some persons, in their hatred of discipline, recoil from its very name, let them understand this: if no society, indeed, no house which has even a small family, can be kept in proper condition without discipline, it is much more necessary in the church, whose condition should be as ordered as possible. Accordingly, as the saving doctrine of Christ is the soul of the church, so does discipline serve as its sinews, through which the members of the body hold together, each in its own place. Therefore, all who desire to remove discipline or to hinder its restoration—whether they do this deliberately or out of ignorance—are surely contributing to the ultimate dissolution of the church. For what will happen if each is allowed to do what he pleases? Yet that would happen, if to the preaching of doctrine there were not added private admonitions, corrections, and other aids of the sort that sustain doctrine and do not let it remain idle. Therefore, discipline is like a bridle to restrain and tame those who rage against the doctrine of Christ; or like a spur to arouse those of little inclination; and also sometimes like a father's rod to chastise mildly and with the gentleness of Christ's Spirit those who have more seriously lapsed.

Stages of church discipline   4.12.2

The first foundation of discipline is to provide a place for private admonition; that is, if anyone does not perform his duty willingly, or behaves insolently, or does not live honorably, or has committed any act deserving blame—he should allow himself to be admonished; and when the situation demands it, every man should endeavor to admonish his brother. But let pastors and presbyters be especially watchful to do this, for their duty is not only to preach to the people, but to warn and exhort in every house, wherever they are not effective enough in general instruction.

The handling of church discipline in the various cases   4.12.6

It remains for us to see how the church carries out this part of discipline which falls within its jurisdiction. To begin with, let us keep the division set forth above: that some sins are public; others, private or somewhat secret. Public sins are those witnessed not by one or two persons, but committed openly and to the offense of the entire church. I call secret sins, not those completely hidden from men, as are those of hypocrites (for these do not fall under the judgment of the church), but those of an intermediate sort, which are not unwitnessed, yet not public.

But we ought not to pass over the fact that such severity as is joined with a "spirit of gentleness" [Gal. 6:1] befits the church. For we must always, as Paul bids us, take particular care that he who is punished be not overwhelmed with sorrow [II Cor. 2:7]. Thus a remedy would become destruction. But, from the purpose intended it would be better to take a rule of moderation. For, in excommunication the intent is to lead the sinner to repentance and to remove bad examples from the midst, lest either Christ's name be maligned or others be provoked to imitate them. If, then, we look to these things, it will be easy for us to judge how far severity ought to go and where it ought to stop. Therefore, when a sinner gives testimony of his repentance to the church, and by this testimony wipes out the offense as far as he can, he is not to be urged any further. If he is so urged, the rigor will now exceed due measure.... Chrysostom ... speaks as follows: "If God is so kind, why does his priest wish to seem so rigorous?" We know, moreover, what gentleness Augustine used toward the Donatists. He did not hesitate to take back to their bishoprics those who had returned from schism, and that immediately after repentance!

The Sacraments

(The word "sacrament" explained:
sacraments are signs of God's covenants)

Definition

First, we must consider what a sacrament is. It seems to me that a simple and proper definition would be to say that it is an outward sign by which the Lord seals on our consciences the promises of his good will toward us in order to sustain the weakness of our faith; and we in turn attest our piety toward him in the presence of the Lord and of his angels and before men. Here is another briefer definition: one may call it a testimony of divine grace toward us, confirmed by an outward sign, with mutual attestation of our piety toward him. Whichever of these definitions you may choose, it does not differ in meaning from that of Augustine, who teaches that a sacrament is "a visible sign of a sacred thing," or "a visible form of an invisible grace."

Word and sign

Now, from the definition that I have set forth we understand that a sacrament is never without a preceding promise but is joined to it as a sort of appendix, with the purpose of confirming and sealing the promise itself, and of making it more evident to us and in a sense ratifying it. By this means God provides first for our ignorance and dullness, then for our weakness. Yet, properly speaking, it is not so much needed to confirm his Sacred Word as to establish us in faith in it. For God's truth is of itself firm and sure enough, and it cannot receive better confirmation from any other source than from itself. But as our faith is slight and feeble unless it be propped on all sides and sustained by every means, it trembles, wavers, totters, and at last gives way. Here our merciful Lord, according to his infinite kindness, so tempers himself to our capacity that, since we are creatures who always creep on the ground, cleave to the flesh, and, do not think about or even conceive of anything spiritual, he condescends to lead us to himself even by these earthly elements, and to set before us in the flesh a mirror of spiritual blessings.

The word must explain the sign

What our opponents commonly say is this: a sacrament consists of the word and the outward sign. For we ought to understand the word not as one whispered without meaning and without faith, a mere noise, like a magic incantation, which has the force to consecrate the element. Rather, it should, when preached, make us understand what the visible sign means.... You see how the sacrament requires preaching to beget faith.

4.14.7–13   *(They confirm faith, not of themselves, but as agencies of the Holy Spirit and in association with the Word; and they are distinguishing marks of our profession of faith before men)*

4.14.7   *The reception of the sacraments by the wicked is no evidence against their importance*

It is therefore certain that the Lord offers us mercy and the pledge of his grace both in his Sacred Word and in his sacraments. But it is understood only by those who take Word and sacraments with sure faith, just as Christ is offered and held forth by the Father to all unto salvation, yet not all acknowledge and receive him. In one place Augustine, meaning to convey this, said that the efficacy of the Word is brought to light in the sacrament, not because it is spoken, but because it is believed.

4.14.9   *The Holy Spirit in the sacraments*

But the sacraments properly fulfill their office only when the Spirit, that inward teacher, comes to them, by whose power alone hearts are penetrated and affections moved and our souls opened for the sacraments to enter in. If the Spirit be lacking, the sacraments can accomplish nothing more in our minds than the splendor of the sun shining upon blind eyes, or a voice sounding in deaf ears. Therefore, I make such a division between Spirit and sacraments that the power to act rests with the former, and the ministry alone is left to the latter—a ministry empty and trifling, apart from the action of the Spirit, but charged with great effect when the Spirit works within and manifests his power.

4.14.12   *Sacramental elements have value only as God's instruments*

To their other objection—that the glory of God passes down to the creatures, and so much power is attributed to them, and is thus to this extent diminished—our answer is ready: we place no power in creatures. I say only this: God uses means and instruments which he himself sees to be expedient, that all things may serve his glory, since he is Lord and Judge of all. He feeds our bodies through bread and other foods, he illumines the world through the sun, and he warms it through heat; yet neither bread, nor sun, nor fire, is anything save in so far as he distributes his blessings to us by these instruments. In like manner, he nourishes faith spiritually through the sacraments, whose one function is to set his promises before our eyes to be looked upon, indeed, to be guarantees of them to us.

(They do not of themselves impart grace,   4.14.14–17
but, like the Word, hold forth Christ)

The sacraments have significance for us in faith in Christ   4.14.16

I say that Christ is the matter or (if you prefer) the substance of all the sacraments; for in him they have all their firmness, and they do not promise anything apart from him.

True office of the sacraments   4.14.17

Let it be regarded as a settled principle that the sacraments have the same office as the Word of God: to offer and set forth Christ to us, and in him the treasures of heavenly grace. But they avail and profit nothing unless received in faith. . . . God therefore truly executes whatever he promises and represents in signs; nor do the signs lack their own effect in proving their Author truthful and faithful. The only question here is whether God acts by his own intrinsic power (as they say) or resigns his office to outward symbols. But we contend that, whatever instruments he uses, these detract nothing from his original activity.

(Wide application of the term to Scriptural incidents   4.14.18–20
and its restriction to the ordinary sacraments of the church)

Christ promised in the Old Testament sacraments   4.14.20

The sacraments themselves were also diverse, in keeping with the times, according to the dispensation by which the Lord was pleased to reveal himself in various ways to men. For circumcision was enjoined upon Abraham and his descendants [Gen. 17:10]. To it were afterward added purifications [Lev., chs. 11 to 15], sacrifices, and other rites [Lev., chs. 1 to 10] from the law of Moses. These were the sacraments of the Jews until the coming of Christ. When at his coming these were abrogated, two sacraments were instituted which the Christian church now uses, Baptism and the Lord's Supper. . . .

Yet those ancient sacraments looked to the same purpose to which ours now tend: to direct and almost lead men by the hand to Christ, or rather, as images, to represent him and show him forth to be known. We have already taught that they are seals by which God's promises are sealed, and, moreover, it is very clear that no promise has ever been offered to men except in Christ [II Cor. 1:20]. Consequently, to teach us about any promise of God, they must show forth Christ.

4.14.21–6   *(Sacraments of the Old Testament closely related to those of the New as foreshadowing the full manifestation of Christ)*

4.15   BAPTISM

4.15.1–6   *(Baptism a sign of our forgiveness, of our participation in Christ's death and resurrection and also in his blessing)*

4.15.1   *The meaning of baptism*

Baptism is the sign of the initiation by which we are received into the society of the church, in order that, engrafted in Christ, we may be reckoned among God's children. Now baptism was given to us by God for these ends (which I have taught to be common to all sacraments): first, to serve our faith before him; secondly, to serve our confession before men. We shall treat in order the reasons for each aspect of its institution. Baptism brings three things to our faith which we must deal with individually. The first thing that the Lord sets out for us is that baptism should be a token and proof of our cleansing; or (the better to explain what I mean) it is like a sealed document to confirm to us that all our sins are so abolished, remitted, and effaced that they can never come to his sight, be recalled, or charged against us. For he wills that all who believe be baptized for the remission of sins [Matt. 28:19; Acts 2:38].

Accordingly, they who regarded baptism as nothing but a token and mark by which we confess our religion before men, as soldiers bear the insignia of their commander as a mark of their profession, have not weighed what was the chief point of baptism. It is to receive baptism with this promise: "He who believes and is baptized will be saved" [Mark 16:16].

4.15.2   *Its virtue not in water without the Word*

Baptism promises us no other purification than through the sprinkling of Christ's blood, which is represented by means of water from the resemblance to cleansing and washing. Who, therefore, may say that we are cleansed by this water which attests with certainty that Christ's blood is our true and only laver? Thus, the surest argument to refute the self-deception of those who attribute everything to the power of the water can be sought in the meaning of baptism itself, which draws us away, not only from the visible element which meets our eyes, but from all other means, that it may fasten our minds upon Christ alone.

Token of cleansing for the whole of life!

But we are not to think that baptism was conferred upon us only for past time, so that for newly committed sins into which we fall after baptism we must seek new remedies of expiation in some other sacraments, as if the force of the former one were spent. In early times this error caused some to refuse the initiation by baptism unless in uttermost peril of life and at their last gasp, so that thus they might obtain pardon for their whole life. The ancient bishops frequently inveighed in their writings against this preposterous caution. But we must realize that at whatever time we are baptized, we are once for all washed and purged for our whole life. Therefore, as often as we fall away, we ought to recall the memory of our baptism and fortify our mind with it, that we may always be sure and confident of the forgiveness of sins. For, though baptism, administered only once, seemed to have passed, it was still not destroyed by subsequent sins. For Christ's purity has been offered us in it; his purity ever flourishes; it is defiled by no spots, but buries and cleanses away all our defilements.

Nevertheless, from this fact we ought not to take leave to sin in the future, as this has certainly not taught us to be so bold. Rather, this doctrine is only given to sinners who groan, wearied and oppressed by their own sins, in order that they may have something to lift them up and comfort them, so as not to plunge into confusion and despair. Paul speaks thus: "Christ was made our expiator for the forgiveness of past sins" [Rom. 3:25].

True relation of baptism and repentance

Therefore, there is no doubt that all pious folk throughout life, whenever they are troubled by a consciousness of their faults, may venture to remind themselves of their baptism, that from it they may be confirmed in assurance of that sole and perpetual cleansing which we have in Christ's blood.

Baptism as token of mortification and renewal in Christ

Baptism also brings another benefit, for it shows us our mortification in Christ, and new life in him. Indeed (as the apostle says), "we have been baptized into his death," "buried with him into death, . . . that we may walk in newness of life" [Rom. 6:3–4 p.]. By these words he not only exhorts us to follow Christ as if he had said that we are admonished through baptism to die to our desires by an example of Christ's death, and to be aroused to righteousness by the example of his resurrection. But he also takes hold of something far higher, namely, that through baptism Christ makes us sharers in his death, that we may be engrafted in it [Rom. 6:5, cf. Vg.]. And, just as the twig draws substance and nourishment from the root to which it is grafted, so those who receive baptism with right faith truly feel the effective working of Christ's death in the mortification of their flesh, together with the working of his resurrection in the vivification of the Spirit [Rom. 6:8]. . . . Thus, the free pardon of sins and the imputation of righteousness are first promised us, and then the grace of the Holy Spirit to reform us to newness of life.

4.15.6   *Baptism as token of our union with Christ*

Lastly, our faith receives from baptism the advantage of its sure testimony to us that we are not only engrafted into the death and life of Christ, but so united to Christ himself that we become sharers in all his blessings. For he dedicated and sanctified baptism in his own body [Matt. 3:13] in order that he might have it in common with us as the firmest bond of the union and fellowship which he has deigned to form with us. Hence, Paul proves that we are children of God from the fact that we put on Christ in baptism [Gal. 3:26–27]. Thus we see that the fulfillment of baptism is in Christ, whom also for this reason we call the proper object of baptism. Consequently, it is not strange that the apostles are reported to have baptized in his name [Acts 8:16; 19:5], although they had also been bidden to baptize in the name of the Father and of the Spirit [Matt. 28:19]. For all the gifts of God proffered in baptism are found in Christ alone. Yet this cannot take place unless he who baptizes in Christ invokes also the names of the Father and the Spirit. For we are cleansed by his blood because our merciful Father, wishing to receive us into grace in accordance with his incomparable kindness, has set this Mediator among us to gain favor for us in his sight. But we obtain regeneration by Christ's death and resurrection only if we are sanctified by the Spirit and imbued with a new and spiritual nature. For this reason we obtain and, so to speak, clearly discern in the Father the cause, in the Son the matter, and in the Spirit the effect, of our purgation and our regeneration. So John first baptized, so later did the apostles, "with a baptism of repentance unto forgiveness of sins" [Matt. 3:6, 11; Luke 3:16; John 3:23; 4:1; Acts

2:38, 41]—meaning by the word "repentance" such regeneration; and by "forgiveness of sins," cleansing.

(The baptism of John not different from that of the apostles: its meaning symbolized to the Israelites in the exodus)   4.15.7–9

(We are not by the rite of baptism set free from original sin, but by it we make confession of faith before men)   4.15.10–13

Baptism, original sin, and new righteousness   4.15.10

Now, it is clear how false is the teaching, long propagated by some and still persisted in by others, that through baptism we are released and made exempt from original sin, and from the corruption that descended from Adam into all his posterity; and are restored into that same righteousness and purity of nature which Adam would have obtained if he had remained upright as he was first created. For teachers of this type never understood what original sin, what original righteousness, or what the grace of baptism was. But we have already contended that original sin is the depravity and corruption of our nature, which first renders us liable to God's wrath, then also gives rise to what Scripture calls "works of the flesh" [Gal. 5:19]. We must therefore carefully note these two points.

As we are vitiated and corrupted in all parts of our nature, we are held rightly condemned on account of such corruption alone and convicted before God, to whom nothing is acceptable but righteousness, innocence, and purity. Even infants bear their condemnation with them from their mother's womb; for, though they have not yet brought forth the fruits of their own iniquity, they have the seed enclosed within themselves. Indeed, their whole nature is a seed of sin; thus it cannot but be hateful and abominable to God. Through baptism, believers are assured that this condemnation has been removed and withdrawn from them, since (as was said) the Lord promises us by this sign that full and complete remission has been made, both of the guilt that should have been imputed to us, and of the punishment that we ought to have undergone because of the guilt. They also lay hold on righteousness, but such righteousness as the people of God can obtain in this life, that is, by imputation only, since the Lord of his own mercy considers them righteous and innocent.

Baptism as token of confession   4.15.13

But baptism serves as our confession before men. Indeed, it is the mark by which we publicly profess that we wish to be reckoned

God's people; by which we testify that we agree in worshiping the same God, in one religion with all Christians; by which finally we openly affirm our faith. Thus not only do our hearts breathe the praise of God, but our tongues also and all members of our body resound his praise in every way they can.

4.15.14–18　　*(Baptism to be received with trust in the promise of which it is a sign, and not repeated)*

4.15.14　　*Sign and thing*

We ought to deem it certain and proved that it is he who speaks to us through the sign; that it is he who purifies and washes away sins, and wipes out the remembrance of them; that it is he who makes us sharers in his death, who deprives Satan of his rule, who weakens the power of our lust; indeed, that it is he who comes into a unity with us so that, having put on Christ, we may be acknowledged God's children. These things, I say, he performs for our soul within as truly and surely as we see our body outwardly cleansed, submerged, and surrounded with water. For this analogy or similitude is the surest rule of the sacraments: that we should see spiritual things in physical, as if set before our very eyes. For the Lord was pleased to represent them by such figures—not because such graces are bound and enclosed in the sacrament so as to be conferred upon us by its power, but only because the Lord by this token attests his will toward us, namely, that he is pleased to lavish all these things upon us. And he does not feed our eyes with a mere appearance only, but leads us to the present reality and effectively performs what it symbolizes.

4.15.15　　*Baptism as confirming faith*

But from this sacrament, as from all others, we obtain only as much as we receive in faith. If we lack faith, this will be evidence of our ungratefulness, which renders us chargeable before God, because we have not believed the promise given there.

But as far as it is a symbol of our confession, we ought by it to testify that our confidence is in God's mercy, and our purity in forgiveness of sins, which has been procured for us through Jesus Christ; and that we enter God's church in order to live harmoniously with all believers in complete agreement of faith and love. This last point was what Paul meant when he said, "We have all been baptized in one Spirit that we may be one body" [I Cor. 12:13 p.].

4.15.19–21　　*(Objections to ceremonial accretions and to baptism by women)*

Erroneous and correct baptismal usage   4.15.19

But whether the person being baptized should be wholly immersed, and whether thrice or once, whether he should only be sprinkled with poured water—these details are of no importance, but ought to be optional to churches according to the diversity of countries. Yet the word "baptize" means to immerse, and it is clear that the rite of immersion was observed in the ancient church.

Zipporah's circumcision of her son no precedent for baptism by women   4.15.22

Infants are not barred from the Kingdom of Heaven just because they happen to depart the present life before they have been immersed in water. Yet we have already seen that serious injustice is done to God's covenant if we do not assent to it, as if it were weak of itself, since its effect depends neither upon baptism nor upon any additions. Afterward, a sort of seal is added to the sacrament, not to confer efficacy upon God's promise as if it were invalid of itself, but only to confirm it to us. From this it follows that the children of believers are baptized not in order that they who were previously strangers to the church may then for the first time become children of God, but rather that, because by the blessing of the promise they already belonged to the body of Christ, they are received into the church with this solemn sign.

INFANT BAPTISM BEST ACCORDS WITH CHRIST'S INSTITUTION   4.16
AND THE NATURE OF THE SIGN

(Infant baptism, considered in relation to what it typifies, corresponds   4.16.1–6
to circumcision and is authorized in the covenant with Abraham)

The difference is in externals only   4.16.4

Circumcision was for the Jews their first entry into the church, because it was a token to them by which they were assured of adoption as the people and household of God, and they in turn professed to enlist in God's service. In like manner, we also are consecrated to God through baptism, to be reckoned as his people, and in turn we swear fealty to him. By this it appears incontrovertible that baptism has taken the place of circumcision to fulfill the same office among us.

Difference in the mode of confirmation only   4.16.6

For the time of the Old Testament he instituted circumcision to confirm his covenant, but that after circumcision was abolished, the same reason for confirming his covenant (which we have in common with the Jews) still holds good. Consequently, we must always diligently consider what is common to both, and what they have apart from us. The covenant is common, and the reason for confirming it is common. Only the manner of confirmation is different—what was circumcision for them was replaced for us by baptism.

4.16.7–9   *(Christ invited and blessed little children: we should not exclude them from the sign, and the benefit, of baptism)*

4.16.9   *The blessing of infant baptism*

If anyone should object that the promise ought to be enough to confirm the salvation of our children, I disregard this argument. For God views this otherwise; as he perceives our weakness, so he has willed to deal tenderly with us in this matter. Accordingly, let those who embrace the promise that God's mercy is to be extended to their children deem it their duty to offer them to the church to be sealed by the symbol of mercy, and thereby to arouse themselves to a surer confidence, because they see with their very eyes the covenant of the Lord engraved upon the bodies of their children.

4.16.10–16   *(Answer to the Anabaptist argument that baptism is not to be associated with circumcision)*

4.16.17–20   *(Answer to the argument that infants are incapable of faith)*

4.16.20   *Objection: infants are capable neither of repentance nor of faith*

Infants are baptized into future repentance and faith, and even though these have not yet been formed in them, the seed of both lies hidden within them by the secret working of the Spirit.

4.16.21–22   *(Operation of the Spirit in baptized children)*

4.16.21   *The child grows into an understanding of his baptism*

In infant baptism nothing more of present effectiveness must be required than to confirm and ratify the covenant made with them by the Lord. The remaining significance of this sacrament will afterward follow at such time as God himself foresees.

4.16.23–24   *(Infant baptism in the beginning of the church)*

4.16.25–30   *(Certain passages adduced against infant baptism interpreted: those who die unbaptized not all condemned)*

Baptism and Lord's Supper

If we consider the peculiar character of baptism, surely it is an entrance and a sort of initiation into the church, through which we are numbered among God's people: a sign of our spiritual regeneration, through which we are reborn as children of God. On the other hand, the Supper is given to older persons who, having passed tender infancy, can now take solid food.

(Answers to arguments of Servetus, and conclusion)   4.16.31–32

Gratitude due for God's care of our children

For how sweet is it to godly minds to be assured, not only by word, but by sight, that they obtain so much favor with the Heavenly Father that their offspring are within his care? For here we can see how he takes on toward us the role of a most provident Father, who even after our death maintains his care for us, providing for and looking after our children. . . . Accordingly, unless we wish spitefully to obscure God's goodness, let us offer our infants to him, for he gives them a place among those of his family and household, that is, the members of the church.

THE SACRED SUPPER OF CHRIST, AND WHAT IT BRINGS TO US   4.17

(The Lord's Supper, with the signs of bread and wine, provides spiritual food)   4.17.1–3

Sign and thing

God has received us, once for all, into his family, to hold us not only as servants but as sons. Thereafter, to fulfill the duties of a most excellent Father concerned for his offspring, he undertakes also to nourish us throughout the course of our life. And not content with this alone, he has willed, by giving his pledge, to assure us of this continuing liberality. To this end, therefore, he has, through the hand of his only-begotten Son, given to his church another sacrament, that is, a spiritual banquet, wherein Christ attests himself to be the life-giving bread, upon which our souls feed unto true and blessed immortality [John 6:51]. . . .

First, the signs are bread and wine, which represent for us the invisible food that we receive from the flesh and blood of Christ. For as in baptism, God, regenerating us, engrafts us into the society of his church and makes us his own by adoption, so we have said, that he discharges the function of a provident householder in continually supplying to us the food to sustain and preserve us in that life into which he has begotten us by his Word.

Now Christ is the only food of our soul, and therefore our Heavenly Father invites us to Christ, that, refreshed by partaking of him, we may repeatedly gather strength until we shall have reached heavenly immortality. Since, however, this mystery of Christ's secret union with the devout is by nature incomprehensible, he shows its figure and image in visible signs best adapted to our small capacity. Indeed, by giving guarantees and tokens he makes it as certain for us as if we had seen it with our own eyes. For this very familiar comparison penetrates into even the dullest minds: just as bread and wine sustain physical life, so are souls fed by Christ. We now understand the purpose of this mystical blessing, namely, to confirm for us the fact that the Lord's body was once for all so sacrificed for us that we may now feed upon it, and by feeding feel in ourselves the working of that unique sacrifice; and that his blood was once so shed for us in order to be our perpetual drink.

4.17.2 *Union with Christ as the special fruit of the Lord's Supper*

Godly souls can gather great assurance and delight from this Sacrament; in it they have a witness of our growth into one body with Christ such that whatever is his may be called ours. As a consequence, we may dare assure ourselves that eternal life, of which he is the heir, is ours; and that the Kingdom of Heaven, into which he has already entered, can no more be cut off from us than from him; again, that we cannot be condemned for our sins, from whose guilt he has absolved us, since he willed to take them upon himself as if they were his own. This is the wonderful exchange which, out of his measureless benevolence, he has made with us; that, becoming Son of man with us, he has made us sons of God with him; that, by his descent to earth, he has prepared an ascent to heaven for us; that, by taking on our mortality, he has conferred his immortality upon us; that, accepting our weakness, he has strengthened us by his power; that, receiving our poverty unto himself, he has transferred his wealth to us; that, taking the weight of our iniquity upon himself (which oppressed us), he has clothed us with his righteousness.

4.17.3 *The spiritual presence of Christ*

In this Sacrament we have such full witness of all these things that we must certainly consider them as if Christ here present were himself set before our eyes and touched by our hands. . . .

We must carefully observe that the very powerful and almost entire force of the Sacrament lies in these words: "which is given for you," "which is shed for you." The present distribution of the body and blood of the Lord would not greatly benefit us unless they had once for all been given for our redemption and salvation. They are therefore represented under bread and wine so that we may learn not only that they are ours but that they have been destined as food for our spiritual life. And so as we previously stated, from the physical things set forth in the Sacrament we are led by a sort of analogy to spiritual things. Thus, when bread is given as a symbol of Christ's body, we must at once grasp this comparison: as bread nourishes, sustains, and keeps the life of our body, so Christ's body is the only food to invigorate and enliven our soul. When we see wine set forth as a symbol of blood, we must reflect on the benefits which wine imparts to the body, and so realize that the same are spiritually imparted to us by Christ's blood. These benefits are to nourish, refresh, strengthen, and gladden. For if we sufficiently consider what value we have received from the giving of that most holy body and the shedding of that blood, we shall clearly perceive that those qualities of bread and wine are, according to such an analogy, excellently adapted to express those things when they are communicated to us.

(The promise sealed in the Supper as we are made partakers   4.17.4–7
of Christ's flesh—a mystery felt rather than explained)

The meaning of the promise of the Lord's Supper   4.17.4

It is not, therefore, the chief function of the Sacrament simply and without higher consideration to extend to us the body of Christ. Rather, it is to seal and confirm that promise by which he testifies that his flesh is food indeed and his blood is drink [John 6:56], which feed us unto eternal life [John 6:55]. By this he declares himself to be the bread of life, of which he who eats will live forever [John 6:48, 50]. And to do this, the Sacrament sends us to the cross of Christ, where that promise was indeed performed and in all respects fulfilled. For we do not eat Christ duly and unto salvation unless he is crucified, when in living experience we grasp the efficacy of his death.

How we are partakers by faith   4.17.5

Once for all, therefore, he gave his body to be made bread when he yielded himself to be crucified for the redemption of the world; daily he gives it when by the word of the gospel he offers it for us to partake, inasmuch as it was crucified, when he seals such giving of himself by the sacred mystery of the Supper, and when he inwardly fulfills what he outwardly designates.

Now here we ought to guard against two faults. First, we should not, by too little regard for the signs, divorce them from their mysteries, to which they are so to speak attached. Secondly, we should not, by extolling them immoderately, seem to obscure somewhat the mysteries themselves.

We admit indeed, meanwhile, that this is no other eating than that of faith, as no other can be imagined. But here is the difference between my words and theirs: for them to eat is only to believe; I say that we eat Christ's flesh in believing, because it is made ours by faith, and that this eating is the result and effect of faith. Or if you want it said more clearly, for them eating is faith; for me it seems rather to follow from faith. . . . In this way the Lord intended, by calling himself the "bread of life" [John 6:51], to teach not only that salvation for us rests on faith in his death and resurrection, but also that, by true partaking of him, his life passes into us and is made ours—just as bread when taken as food imparts vigor to the body.

4.17.8–10   *(This life-giving communion is brought about by the Holy Spirit)*

4.17.10   *The presence of Christ's body in the Lord's Supper*

Even though it seems unbelievable that Christ's flesh, separated from us by such great distance, penetrates to us, so that it becomes our food, let us remember how far the secret power of the Holy Spirit towers above all our senses, and how foolish it is to wish to measure his immeasurableness by our measure. What, then, our mind does not comprehend, let faith conceive: that the Spirit truly unites things separated in space. . . .

I indeed admit that the breaking of bread is a symbol; it is not the thing itself. But, having admitted this, we shall nevertheless duly infer that by the showing of the symbol the thing itself is also shown. For unless a man means to call God a deceiver, he would never dare assert that an empty symbol is set forth by him. Therefore, if the Lord truly represents the participation in his body through the breaking of bread, there ought not to be the least doubt that he truly presents and shows his body. And the godly ought by all means to keep this rule: whenever they see symbols appointed by the Lord, to think and be persuaded that the truth of the thing signified is surely present there. For why should the Lord put in your hand the symbol of his body, except to assure you of a true participation in it? But if it is true that a visible sign is given us to seal the gift of a thing invisible, when we have received the symbol of the body, let us no less surely trust that the body itself is also given to us.

(Relation of the outward sign and invisible reality variously   4.17.11–15
misstated by the Schoolmen, and in the doctrine of transubstantiation)

Signification, matter, and effect of the Sacrament   4.17.11

I therefore say (what has always been accepted in the church and is today taught by all of sound opinion) that the sacred mystery of the Supper consists in two things: physical signs, which, thrust before our eyes, represent to us, according to our feeble capacity, things invisible; and spiritual truth, which is at the same time represented and displayed through the symbols themselves.

When I wish to show the nature of this truth in familiar terms, I usually set down three things: the signification, the matter that depends upon it, and the power or effect that follows from both. The signification is contained in the promises, which are, so to speak, implicit in the sign. I call Christ with his death and resurrection the matter, or substance. But by effect I understand redemption, righteousness, sanctification, and eternal life, and all the other benefits Christ gives to us. . . .

I say, therefore, that in the mystery of the Supper, Christ is truly shown to us through the symbols of bread and wine, his very body and blood, in which he has fulfilled all obedience to obtain righteousness for us. Why? First, that we may grow into one body with him; secondly, having been made partakers of his substance, that we may also feel his power in partaking of all his benefits.

(Arguments for rejection of the doctrine of the ubiquity of the body   4.17.16–31
as narrowly literal, together with exposition of the spiritual view
of communion with Christ in heaven)

How is the presence of Christ in the Lord's Supper to be thought of?   4.17.19

But we must establish such a presence of Christ in the Supper as may neither fasten him to the element of bread, nor enclose him in bread, nor circumscribe him in any way (all which things, it is clear, detract from his heavenly glory); finally, such as may not take from him his own stature, or parcel him out to many places at once, or invest him with boundless magnitude to be spread through heaven and earth. For these things are plainly in conflict with a nature truly human. Let us never (I say) allow these two limitations to be taken away from us: (1) Let nothing be withdrawn from Christ's heavenly glory—as happens when he is brought under the corruptible elements of this world, or bound to any earthly creatures. (2) Let nothing inappropriate to human nature be ascribed to his body, as happens when it is said either to be infinite or to be put in a number of places at once.

4.17.31   *Christ not brought down to us; we are lifted up to him*

Greatly mistaken are those who conceive no presence of flesh in the Supper unless it lies in the bread. For thus they leave nothing to the secret working of the Spirit, which unites Christ himself to us. To them Christ does not seem present unless he comes down to us. As though, if he should lift us to himself, we should not just as much enjoy his presence! The question is therefore only of the manner, for they place Christ in the bread, while we do not think it lawful for us to drag him from heaven. Let our readers decide which one is more correct. Only away with that calumny that Christ is removed from his Supper unless he lies hidden under the covering of bread! For since this mystery is heavenly, there is no need to draw Christ to earth that he may be joined to us.

4.17.32–34   *(The true nature of the corporeal presence
in which believers partake through the Spirit)*

4.17.32   *Involved solutions of the mystery rejected*

Now, if anyone should ask me how this takes place, I shall not be ashamed to confess that it is a secret too lofty for either my mind to comprehend or my words to declare. And, to speak more plainly, I rather experience than understand it. Therefore, I here embrace without controversy the truth of God in which I may safely rest. He declares his flesh the food of my soul, his blood its drink [John 6:53 ff.]. I offer my soul to him to be fed with such food. In his Sacred Supper he bids me take, eat, and drink his body and blood under the symbols of bread and wine. I do not doubt that he himself truly presents them, and that I receive them.

4.17.33   *Spiritual and, hence, actual partaking of Christ;
partaking of the Lord's Supper by unbelievers*

They falsely boast that all we teach of spiritual eating is contrary, as they say, to true and real eating, seeing that we pay attention only to the manner, which with them is carnal, while they enclose Christ in bread. For us the manner is spiritual because the secret power of the Spirit is the bond of our union with Christ.

Their other objection is no truer: that we touch only upon the benefit or effect which believers receive from eating Christ's flesh. For, as we have previously stated, Christ himself is the matter of the Supper; and the effect follows from the fact that by the sacrifice of his death we are cleansed of sins, by his blood we are washed, and by his resurrection we are raised to the hope of heavenly life.

Others, agreeing with us, that worthiness itself consists in faith and love, still are far in error on the standard itself of worthiness, requiring, as they do, a perfection of faith which cannot at all be attained, and a love equal to that which Christ has shown toward us. But, by so doing, they, like those previously mentioned, drive all men from approaching this most holy Supper. For if their view obtained, no one would receive it except unworthily, since all to a man would be held guilty and convicted of their own imperfection. And it would be excessive stupidity—not to mention foolishness—to require such perfection in receiving the Sacrament as would make the Sacrament void and superfluous. For it is a sacrament ordained not for the perfect, but for the weak and feeble, to awaken, arouse, stimulate, and exercise the feeling of faith and love, indeed, to correct the defect of both.

4.18.19 *Baptism and the Lord's Supper are the only sacraments*

My readers now possess, collected into summary form, almost everything that I thought should be known concerning these two sacraments, whose use has been handed down to the Christian church from the beginning of the New Testament even to the end of the world; that is, that baptism should be, as it were, an entry into the church, and an initiation into faith; but the Supper should be a sort of continual food on which Christ spiritually feeds the household of his believers. Therefore, as there is but one God, one faith, one Christ, and one church, his body; so baptism is but one [Eph. 4:4–6], and is not a thing oft-repeated. But the Supper is repeatedly distributed, that those who have once been drawn into the church may realize that they continually feed upon Christ.

Apart from these two, no other sacrament has been instituted by God, so the church of believers ought to recognize no other; for erecting and establishing new sacraments is not a matter of human choice.

4.19 THE FIVE OTHER CEREMONIES, FALSELY TERMED SACRAMENTS; ALTHOUGH COMMONLY CONSIDERED SACRAMENTS HITHERTO, THEY ARE PROVED NOT TO BE SUCH, AND THEIR REAL NATURE IS SHOWN

4.19.1–3 *(Five alleged sacraments, not authorized by God's Word or used in the early church)*

4.19.4–13 *(Confirmation not a sacrament: early practice of reception after instruction should be restored)*

4.19.14–17 *(Penance fails to answer the definition of a sacrament)*

4.19.18–21 *(Extreme unction rests upon a misuse of James 5:14–15 and is no sacrament)*

4.19.22–33 *(The alleged sacrament of holy orders complicated by the seven ranks of clergy; the ceremonies of institution and functions of these criticized)*

4.19.34–37 *(Erroneous claim that marriage is a sacrament from misunderstanding of Eph. 5:28 and other passages: abuses connected with marriage)*

4.20 CIVIL GOVERNMENT

4.20.1–2 *(How civil and spiritual government are related)*

Differences between spiritual and civil government

Now, since we have established above that man is under a twofold government, and since we have elsewhere discussed at sufficient length the kind that resides in the soul or inner man and pertains to eternal life, this is the place to say something also about the other kind, which pertains only to the establishment of civil justice and outward morality.

For although this topic seems by nature alien to the spiritual doctrine of faith which I have undertaken to discuss, what follows will show that I am right in joining them, in fact, that necessity compels me to do so. This is especially true since, from one side, insane and barbarous men furiously strive to overturn this divinely established order; while, on the other side, the flatterers of princes, immoderately praising their power, do not hesitate to set them against the rule of God himself. Unless both these evils are checked, purity of faith will perish. Besides, it is of no slight importance to us to know how lovingly God has provided in this respect for mankind, that greater zeal for piety may flourish in us to attest our gratefulness.

The two "governments" are not antithetical

Yet this distinction does not lead us to consider the whole nature of government a thing polluted, which has nothing to do with Christian men. That is what, indeed, certain fanatics who delight in unbridled license shout and boast: after we have died through Christ to the elements of this world [Col. 2:20], are transported to God's Kingdom, and sit among heavenly beings, it is a thing unworthy of us and set far beneath our excellence to be occupied with those vile and worldly cares which have to do with business foreign to a Christian man. To what purpose, they ask, are there laws without trials and tribunals? But what has a Christian man to do with trials themselves? Indeed, if it is not lawful to kill, why do we have laws and trials? But as we have just now pointed out that this kind of government is distinct from that spiritual and inward Kingdom of Christ, so we must know that they are not at variance. For spiritual government, indeed, is already initiating in us upon earth certain beginnings of the Heavenly Kingdom, and in this mortal and fleeting life affords a certain forecast of an immortal and incorruptible blessedness. Yet civil government has as its appointed end, so long as we live among men, to cherish and protect the outward worship of God, to defend sound doctrine of piety and the position of the church, to adjust our life to the society of men, to form our social behavior to civil righteousness, to reconcile us with one another, and to promote general peace and tranquillity. All of this I admit to be superfluous, if God's Kingdom, such as it is now among us, wipes out the present life. But if it is God's will that we go as pilgrims upon the earth while we aspire to the true fatherland, and if the pilgrimage requires such helps, those who take these from man deprive him of his very humanity. Our adversaries claim that there ought to be such great perfection in the church of God that its government should suffice for law. But they stupidly imagine such a perfection as can never be found in a community of men. For since the insolence of evil men is so great, their wickedness so stubborn, that it can scarcely be restrained by extremely severe laws, what do we expect them to do if they see that their depravity can go scot-free—when no power can force them to cease from doing evil?

4.20.3–7   *(Necessity and divine sanction of civil government)*

4.20.3   *The chief tasks and burdens of civil government*

Its function among men is no less than that of bread, water, sun, and air; indeed, its place of honor is far more excellent. For it does not merely see to it, as all these serve to do, that men breathe, eat, drink, and are kept warm, even though it surely embraces all these activities when it provides for their living together. It does not, I repeat, look to this only, but also prevents idolatry, sacrilege against God's name, blasphemies against his truth, and other public offenses against religion from arising and spreading among the people; it prevents the public peace from being disturbed; it provides that each man may keep his property safe and sound; that men may carry on blameless intercourse among themselves; that honesty and modesty may be preserved among men. In short, it provides that a public manifestation of religion may exist among Christians, and that humanity be maintained among men.

Let no man be disturbed that I now commit to civil government the duty of rightly establishing religion, which I seem above to have put outside of human decision. For, when I approve of a civil administration that aims to prevent the true religion which is contained in God's law from being openly and with public sacrilege violated and defiled with impunity, I do not here, any more than before, allow men to make laws according to their own decision concerning religion and the worship of God.

But my readers, assisted by the very clarity of the arrangement, will better understand what is to be thought of the whole subject of civil government if we discuss its parts separately. These are three: the magistrate, who is the protector and guardian of the laws; the laws, according to which he governs; the people, who are governed by the laws and obey the magistrate. Let us, then, first look at the office of the magistrate, noting whether it is a lawful calling approved of God; the nature of the office; the extent of its power; then, with what laws a Christian government ought to be governed; and finally, how the laws benefit the people, and what obedience is owed to the magistrate.

The magistracy is ordained by God

4.20.4

The Lord has not only testified that the office of magistrate is approved by and acceptable to him, but he also sets out its dignity with the most honorable titles and marvelously commends it to us. . . .

Accordingly, no one ought to doubt that civil authority is a calling, not only holy and lawful before God, but also the most sacred and by far the most honorable of all callings in the whole life of mortal men.

Magistrates should be faithful as God's deputies

4.20.6

This consideration ought continually to occupy the magistrates themselves, since it can greatly spur them to exercise their office and bring them remarkable comfort to mitigate the difficulties of their task, which are indeed many and burdensome. For what great zeal for uprightness, for prudence, gentleness, self-control, and for innocence ought to be required of themselves by those who know that they have been ordained ministers of divine justice? How will they have the brazenness to admit injustice to their judgment seat, which they are told is the throne of the living God? How will they have the boldness to pronounce an unjust sentence, by that mouth which they know has been appointed an instrument of divine truth? With what conscience will they sign wicked decrees by that hand which they know has been appointed to record the acts of God? To sum up, if they remember that they are vicars of God, they should watch with all care, earnestness, and diligence, to represent in themselves to men some image of divine providence, protection, goodness, benevolence, and justice. . . . [I]f they commit some fault, they are not only wrongdoers to men whom they wickedly trouble, but are also insulting toward God himself, whose most holy judgments they defile [cf. Isa. 3:14–15]. Again, they have the means to comfort themselves greatly when they ponder in themselves that they are occupied not with profane affairs or those alien to a servant of God, but with a most holy office, since they are serving as God's deputies.

4.20.8–13   *(Forms of government, and duties of magistrates.*
           Issues of war and taxation)

4.20.8   *The diversity of forms of government*

Obviously, it would be an idle pastime for men in private life, who are
disqualified from deliberating on the organization of any commonwealth, to dispute over what would be the best kind of government
in that place where they live. Also this question admits of no simple
solution but requires deliberation, since the nature of the discussion
depends largely upon the circumstances. And if you compare the
forms of government among themselves apart from the circumstances, it is not easy to distinguish which one of them excels in usefulness, for they contend on such equal terms. The fall from kingdom
to tyranny is easy; but it is not much more difficult to fall from the
rule of the best men to the faction of a few; yet it is easiest of all to fall
from popular rule to sedition. For if the three forms of government
which the philosophers discuss be considered in themselves, I will
not deny that aristocracy, or a system compounded of aristocracy and
democracy, far excels all others: not indeed of itself, but because it is
very rare for kings so to control themselves that their will never dis-
agrees with what is just and right; or for them to have been endowed
with such great keenness and prudence, that each knows how much
is enough. Therefore, men's fault or failing causes it to be safer and
more bearable for a number to exercise government, so that they may
help one another, teach and admonish one another; and, if one asserts
himself unfairly, there may be a number of censors and masters to
restrain his willfulness. . . . I freely admit that no kind of government
is more happy than one where freedom is regulated with becoming
moderation and is properly established on a durable basis, so also I
reckon most happy those permitted to enjoy this state; and if they
stoutly and constantly labor to preserve and retain it, I grant that they
are doing nothing alien to this office. Indeed, the magistrates ought to
apply themselves with the highest diligence to prevent the freedom
(whose guardians they have been appointed) from being in any
respect diminished, far less be violated. If they are not sufficiently alert
and careful, they are faithless in office, and traitors to their country.

But if those to whom the Lord has appointed another form of government should transfer this very function to themselves, being
moved to desire a change of government—even to think of such a
move will not only be foolish and superfluous, but altogether harmful. However, as you will surely find if you fix your eyes not on one
city alone, but look around and glance at the world as a whole, or at

least cast your sight upon regions farther off, divine providence has wisely arranged that various countries should be ruled by various kinds of government. For as elements cohere only in unequal proportion, so countries are best held together according to their own particular inequality. However, all these things are needlessly spoken to those for whom the will of the Lord is enough. For if it has seemed good to him to set kings over kingdoms, senates or municipal officers over free cities, it is our duty to show ourselves compliant and obedient to whomever he sets over the places where we live.

Concern for both Tables of the Law   4.20.9

We ought to explain in passing the office of the magistrates, how it is described in the Word of God and the things in which it consists. If Scripture did not teach that it extends to both Tables of the Law, we could learn this from secular writers: for no one has discussed the office of magistrates, the making of laws, and public welfare, without beginning at religion and divine worship. And thus all have confessed that no government can be happily established unless piety is the first concern; and that those laws are preposterous which neglect God's right and provide only for men. . . .

As far as the Second Table is concerned, Jeremiah admonishes kings to "do justice and righteousness," to "deliver him who has been oppressed by force from the hand of the oppressor," not to "grieve or wrong the alien, the widow, and the fatherless" or "shed innocent blood" [Jer. 22:3, cf. Vg.]. . . . We see, therefore, that they are ordained protectors and vindicators of public innocence, modesty, decency, and tranquillity, and that their sole endeavor should be to provide for the common safety and peace of all. . . .

Justice, indeed, is to receive into safekeeping, to embrace, to protect, vindicate, and free the innocent. But judgment is to withstand the boldness of the impious, to repress their violence, to punish their misdeeds.

The magistrates' exercise of force is compatible with piety   4.20.10

But here a seemingly hard and difficult question arises: if the law of God forbids all Christians to kill [Ex. 20:13; Deut. 5:17; Matt. 5:21], and the prophet prophesies concerning God's holy mountain (the church) that in it men shall not afflict or hurt [Isa.11:9; 65:25]—how can magistrates be pious men and shedders of blood at the same time?

Yet if we understand that the magistrate in administering punishments does nothing by himself, but carries out the very judgments of

God, we shall not be hampered by this scruple. . . . Yet it is necessary for the magistrate to pay attention to both, lest by excessive severity he either harm more than heal; or, by superstitious affectation of clemency, fall into the cruelest gentleness, if he should (with a soft and dissolute kindness) abandon many to their destruction. For during the reign of Nerva it was not without reason said: it is indeed bad to live under a prince with whom nothing is permitted; but much worse under one by whom everything is allowed.

4.20.11 *On the right of the government to wage war*

But kings and people must sometimes take up arms to execute such public vengeance. On this basis we may judge wars lawful which are so undertaken. For if power has been given them to preserve the tranquillity of their dominion, to restrain the seditious stirrings of restless men, to help those forcibly oppressed, to punish evil deeds—can they use it more opportunely than to check the fury of one who disturbs both the repose of private individuals and the common tranquillity of all, who raises seditious tumults, and by whom violent oppressions and vile misdeeds are perpetrated? If they ought to be the guardians and defenders of the laws, they should also overthrow the efforts of all whose offenses corrupt the discipline of the laws. Indeed, if they rightly punish those robbers whose harmful acts have affected only a few, will they allow a whole country to be afflicted and devastated by robberies with impunity? For it makes no difference whether it be a king or the lowest of the common folk who invades a foreign country in which he has no right, and harries it as an enemy. All such must, equally, be considered as robbers and punished accordingly. Therefore, both natural equity and the nature of the office dictate that princes must be armed not only to restrain the misdeeds of private individuals by judicial punishment, but also to defend by war the dominions entrusted to their safekeeping, if at any time they are under enemy attack. And the Holy Spirit declares such wars to be lawful by many testimonies of Scripture.

4.20.12 *Restraint and humanity in war*

If anyone object against me that in the New Testament there exists no testimony or example which teaches that war is a thing lawful for Christians, I answer first that the reason for waging war which existed of old still persists today; and that, on the other hand, there is no reason that bars magistrates from defending their subjects. Secondly, I say that an express declaration of this matter is not to be sought in the writings of the apostles; for their purpose is not to fashion a civil government, but to establish the spiritual Kingdom of Christ. Finally, that it is there shown in passing that Christ by his coming has changed nothing in this respect. . . .

But it is the duty of all magistrates here to guard particularly against giving vent to their passions even in the slightest degree. Rather, if they have to punish, let them not be carried away with headlong anger, or be seized with hatred, or burn with implacable severity. Let them also (as Augustine says) have pity on the common nature in the one whose special fault they are punishing. Or, if they must arm themselves against the enemy, that is, the armed robber, let them not lightly seek occasion to do so; indeed, let them not accept the occasion when offered, unless they are driven to it by extreme necessity. For if we must perform much more than the heathen philosopher required when he wanted war to seem a seeking of peace, surely everything else ought to be tried before recourse is had to arms. . . .

Moreover, this same right to wage war furnishes the reason for garrisons, leagues, and other civil defenses. Now, I call "garrisons," those troops which are stationed among the cities to defend the boundaries of a country; "leagues," those pacts which are made by neighboring princes to the end that if any trouble should happen in their lands, they may come to one another's aid, and join forces to put down the common enemies of mankind. I call "civil defenses," things used in the art of war.

Concerning the right of the government to levy tribute   4.20.13

Lastly, I also wish to add this, that tributes and taxes are the lawful revenues of princes, which they may chiefly use to meet the public expenses of their office; yet they may similarly use them for the magnificence of their household, which is joined, so to speak, with the dignity of the authority they exercise. . . . Princes themselves will in turn remember that their revenues are not so much their private chests as the treasuries of the entire people (for Paul so testifies [Rom. 13:6]), which cannot be squandered or despoiled without manifest injustice. Or rather, that these are almost the very blood of the people, which it would be the harshest inhumanity not to spare. Moreover, let them consider that their imposts and levies, and other kinds of tributes are nothing but supports of public necessity; but that to impose them upon the common folk without cause is tyrannical extortion. These considerations do not encourage princes to waste and expensive luxury, as there is surely no need to add fuel to their cupidity, already too much kindled of itself.

4.20.14–21   *(Public law and judicial procedures, as related to Christian duty)*

4.20.14   *Old Testament law and the laws of nations*

Next to the magistracy in the civil state come the laws, stoutest sinews of the commonwealth, or, as Cicero, after Plato, calls them, the souls, without which the magistracy cannot stand, even as they themselves have no force apart from the magistracy. Accordingly, nothing truer could be said than that the law is a silent magistrate; the magistrate, a living law.

4.20.18   *The Christian's motives in litigation*

Lawsuits are permissible if rightly used. There is right use, both for the plaintiff in suing and for the accused in defending himself, if the defendant presents himself on the appointed day and with such exception, as he can, defends himself without bitterness, but only with this intent, to defend what is his by right, and if on the other hand, the plaintiff, undeservedly oppressed either in his person or in his property, puts himself in the care of the magistrate, makes his complaint, and seeks what is fair and good. But he should be far from all passion to harm or take revenge, far from harshness and hatred, far from burning desire for contention. He should rather be prepared to yield his own and suffer anything than be carried away with enmity toward his adversary. On the other hand, where hearts are filled with malice, corrupted by envy, inflamed with wrath, breathing revenge, finally so inflamed with desire for contention, that love is somewhat impaired in them, the whole court action of even the most just cause cannot but be impious. For this must be a set principle for all Christians: that a lawsuit, however just, can never be rightly prosecuted by any man, unless he treat his adversary with the same love and good will as if the business under controversy were already amicably settled and composed.

4.20.22–29   *(Obedience, with reverence, due even unjust rulers)*

4.20.22   *Deference*

The first duty of subjects toward their magistrates is to think most honorably of their office, which they recognize as a jurisdiction bestowed by God, and on that account to esteem and reverence them as ministers and representatives of God. . . . I am not discussing the men themselves, as if a mask of dignity covered foolishness, or sloth, or cruelty, as well as wicked morals full of infamous deeds, and thus acquired

for vices the praise of virtues; but I say that the order itself is worthy
of such honor and reverence that those who are rulers are esteemed
among us, and receive reverence out of respect for their lordship.

Obedience   4.20.23

With hearts inclined to reverence their rulers, the subjects should
prove their obedience toward them, whether by obeying their procla-
mations, or by paying taxes, or by undertaking public offices and burdens which pertain to the common defense, or by executing any other
commands of theirs. . . .

[U]nder this obedience I include the restraint which private citizens ought to bid themselves keep in public, that they may not deliberately intrude in public affairs, or pointlessly invade the magistrate's
office, or undertake anything at all politically. If anything in a public
ordinance requires amendment, let them not raise a tumult, or put
their hands to the task—all of them ought to keep their hands bound
in this respect—but let them commit the matter to the judgment of the
magistrate, whose hand alone here is free. I mean, let them not venture on anything without a command. For when the ruler gives his
command, private citizens receive public authority.

Obedience is also due the unjust magistrate   4.20.24

But since we have so far been describing a magistrate who truly is
what he is called, that is, a father of his country, and, as the poet
expresses it, shepherd of his people, guardian of peace, protector of
righteousness, and avenger of innocence—he who does not approve
of such government must rightly be regarded as insane.

But it is the example of nearly all ages that some princes are care-
less about all those things to which they ought to have given heed,
and, far from all care, lazily take their pleasure. Others, intent upon
their own business, put up for sale laws, privileges, judgments, and
letters of favor. Others drain the common people of their money, and
afterward lavish it on insane largesse. Still others exercise sheer rob-
bery, plundering houses, raping virgins and matrons, and slaughter-
ing the innocent.

Consequently, many cannot be persuaded that they ought to recognize these as princes and to obey their authority as far as possible.
For in such great disgrace, and among such crimes, so alien to the
office not only of a magistrate but also of a man, they discern no
appearance of the image of God which ought to have shone in the
magistrate; while they see no trace of that minister of God, who had
been appointed to praise the good, and to punish the evil [cf. 1 Pet.

2:14, Vg.]. Thus, they also do not recognize as ruler him whose dignity and authority Scripture commends to us. Indeed, this inborn feeling has always been in the minds of men to hate and curse tyrants as much as to love and venerate lawful kings.

4.20.25   *The wicked ruler a judgment of God*

But if we look to God's Word, it will lead us farther. We are not only subject to the authority of princes who perform their office toward us uprightly and faithfully as they ought, but also to the authority of all who, by whatever means, have got control of affairs, even though they perform not a whit of the princes' office. For despite the Lord's testimony that the magistrate's office is the highest gift of his beneficence to preserve the safety of men, and despite his appointment of bounds to the magistrates—he still declares at the same time that whoever they may be, they have their authority solely from him. Indeed, he says that those who rule for the public benefit are true patterns and evidences of this beneficence of his; that they who rule unjustly and incompetently have been raised up by him to punish the wickedness of the people; that all equally have been endowed with that holy majesty with which he has invested lawful power.

4.20.29   *It is not the part of subjects but of God to vindicate the right*

We owe this attitude of reverence and therefore of piety toward all our rulers in the highest degree, whatever they may be like. I therefore the more often repeat this: that we should learn not to examine the men themselves, but take it as enough that they bear, by the Lord's will, a character upon which he has imprinted and engraved an inviolable majesty. But (you will say) rulers owe responsibilities in turn to their subjects. This I have already admitted. But if you conclude from this that service ought to be rendered only to just governors, you are reasoning foolishly.

If we are cruelly tormented by a savage prince, if we are greedily despoiled by one who is avaricious or wanton, if we are neglected by a slothful one, if finally we are vexed for piety's sake by one who is impious and sacrilegious, let us first be mindful of our own misdeeds, which without doubt are chastised by such whips of the Lord [cf. Dan. 9:7]. By this, humility will restrain our impatience. Let us then also call this thought to mind, that it is not for us to remedy such evils; that only this remains, to implore the Lord's help, in whose hand are the hearts of kings, and the changing of kingdoms [Prov. 21:1 p.] "He is God who will stand in the assembly of the gods, and will judge in the midst of the gods" [Ps. 82:1 p.].

(Constitutional magistrates, however, ought to check the tyranny of kings; obedience to God comes first)   4.20.30–31

When God intervenes, it is sometimes by unwitting agents   4.20.30

Here are revealed his goodness, his power, and his providence. For sometimes he raises up open avengers from among his servants, and arms them with his command to punish the wicked government and deliver his people, oppressed in unjust ways, from miserable calamity. Sometimes he directs to this end the rage of men with other intentions and other endeavors.

Constitutional defenders of the people's freedom   4.20.31

If there are now any magistrates of the people, appointed to restrain the willfulness of kings (as in ancient times the ephors were set against the Spartan kings, or the tribunes of the people against the Roman consuls, or the demarchs against the senate of the Athenians; and perhaps, as things now are, such power as the three estates exercise in every realm when they hold their chief assemblies), I am so far from forbidding them to withstand, in accordance with their duty, the fierce licentiousness of kings, that, if they wink at kings who violently fall upon and assault the lowly common folk, I declare that their dissimulation involves nefarious perfidy, because they dishonestly betray the freedom of the people, of which they know that they have been appointed protectors by God's ordinance.

Obedience to man must not become disobedience to God   4.20.32

In that obedience which we have shown to be due the authority of rulers, we are always to make this exception, indeed, to observe it as primary, that such obedience is never to lead us away from obedience to him, to whose will the desires of all kings ought to be subject, to whose decrees all their commands ought to yield, to whose majesty their scepters ought to be submitted. And how absurd would it be that in satisfying men you should incur the displeasure of him for whose sake you obey men themselves! The Lord, therefore, is the King of Kings, who, when he has opened his sacred mouth, must alone be heard, before all and above all men; next to him we are subject to those men who are in authority over us, but only in him. If they command anything against him, let it go unesteemed. And here let us not be concerned about all that dignity which the magistrates possess; for no harm is done to it when it is humbled before that singular and truly supreme power of God.

GOD BE PRAISED

Subject Index

175